I0454711

THE NEED FOR THE ESTABLISHMENT OF A PUERTO RICO FINANCIAL STABILITY AND ECONOMIC GROWTH AUTHORITY

OVERSIGHT HEARING

BEFORE THE

SUBCOMMITTEE ON INDIAN, INSULAR AND ALASKA NATIVE AFFAIRS

OF THE

COMMITTEE ON NATURAL RESOURCES U.S. HOUSE OF REPRESENTATIVES

ONE HUNDRED FOURTEENTH CONGRESS

SECOND SESSION

Tuesday, February 2, 2016

Serial No. 114–30

Printed for the use of the Committee on Natural Resources

Available via the World Wide Web: http://www.fdsys.gov
or
Committee address: http://naturalresources.house.gov

U.S. GOVERNMENT PUBLISHING OFFICE

98–458 PDF   WASHINGTON : 2016

For sale by the Superintendent of Documents, U.S. Government Publishing Office
Internet: bookstore.gpo.gov Phone: toll free (866) 512–1800; DC area (202) 512–1800
Fax: (202) 512–2104 Mail: Stop IDCC, Washington, DC 20402–0001

COMMITTEE ON NATURAL RESOURCES

ROB BISHOP, UT, *Chairman*
RAÚL M. GRIJALVA, AZ, *Ranking Democratic Member*

Don Young, AK
Louie Gohmert, TX
Doug Lamborn, CO
Robert J. Wittman, VA
John Fleming, LA
Tom McClintock, CA
Glenn Thompson, PA
Cynthia M. Lummis, WY
Dan Benishek, MI
Jeff Duncan, SC
Paul A. Gosar, AZ
Raúl R. Labrador, ID
Doug LaMalfa, CA
Jeff Denham, CA
Paul Cook, CA
Bruce Westerman, AR
Garret Graves, LA
Dan Newhouse, WA
Ryan K. Zinke, MT
Jody B. Hice, GA
Aumua Amata Coleman Radewagen, AS
Thomas MacArthur, NJ
Alexander X. Mooney, WV
Cresent Hardy, NV
Darin LaHood, IL

Grace F. Napolitano, CA
Madeleine Z. Bordallo, GU
Jim Costa, CA
Gregorio Kilili Camacho Sablan, CNMI
Niki Tsongas, MA
Pedro R. Pierluisi, PR
Jared Huffman, CA
Raul Ruiz, CA
Alan S. Lowenthal, CA
Matt Cartwright, PA
Donald S. Beyer, Jr., VA
Norma J. Torres, CA
Debbie Dingell, MI
Ruben Gallego, AZ
Lois Capps, CA
Jared Polis, CO
Wm. Lacy Clay, MO

Jason Knox, *Chief of Staff*
Lisa Pittman, *Chief Counsel*
David Watkins, *Democratic Staff Director*
Sarah Lim, *Democratic Chief Counsel*

––––––––

SUBCOMMITTEE ON INDIAN, INSULAR AND ALASKA NATIVE AFFAIRS

DON YOUNG, AK, *Chairman*
RAUL RUIZ, CA, *Ranking Democratic Member*

Dan Benishek, MI
Paul A. Gosar, AZ
Doug LaMalfa, CA
Jeff Denham, CA
Paul Cook, CA
Aumua Amata Coleman Radewagen, AS
Rob Bishop, UT, *ex officio*

Madeleine Z. Bordallo, GU
Gregorio Kilili Camacho Sablan, CNMI
Pedro R. Pierluisi, PR
Norma J. Torres, CA
Raúl M. Grijalva, AZ, *ex officio*

––––––––

CONTENTS

OVERSIGHT HEARING ON THE NEED FOR THE ESTABLISHMENT OF A PUERTO RICO FINANCIAL STABILITY AND ECONOMIC GROWTH AUTHORITY

Tuesday, February 2, 2016
U.S. House of Representatives
Subcommittee on Indian, Insular and Alaska Native Affairs
Committee on Natural Resources
Washington, DC

The subcommittee met, pursuant to notice, at 11:01 a.m., in room 1334, Longworth House Office Building, Hon. Don Young [Chairman of the Subcommittee] presiding.

Present: Representatives Young, Denham; Ruiz, Sablan, Pierluisi, Torres, and Grijalva.

Also Present: Representatives Bishop, Labrador, Velazquez, Gutierrez, Serrano, and Gallego.

Mr. YOUNG. The Subcommittee on Indian, Insular and Alaska Native Affairs will come to order. The subcommittee is meeting today to hear testimony on the following oversight topic, "The Need for the Establishment of a Puerto Rico Financial Stability and Economic Growth Authority."

Under Committee Rule 4(f), any oral opening statements at hearings are limited to the Chairman and Ranking Minority Member, and Vice Chairman and Designate of the Ranking Member. This will allow us to hear from the witnesses sooner and help the Members keep to their schedules.

Therefore, I ask unanimous consent that all Members' opening statements be made part of the hearing record when they are submitted to the Subcommittee Clerk by 5:00 p.m. today. Hearing no objections, so ordered.

I also ask unanimous consent that the gentleman from Arizona, Mr. Gallego; and the gentleman from Illinois, Mr. Gutierrez; the gentleman from Idaho, Mr. Labrador; the gentleman from New York, Mr. Serrano; and the gentlewoman from New York, Mrs. Velazquez be allowed to join us on the dais to be recognized and participate in today's hearing. Hearing no objection, so ordered.

STATEMENT OF HON. DON YOUNG, A REPRESENTATIVE IN CONGRESS FROM THE STATE OF ALASKA

Mr. YOUNG. The Subcommittee on Indian, Insular and Alaska Native Affairs meets today again, as I mentioned, on the need for the establishment of a Puerto Rico Financial Stability and Economic Growth Authority. A crisis has gripped the island of Puerto Rico. The Obama administration, Congressional Democrats, the Governor in Puerto Rico, and their local territorial legislation, they are all correct; it is a crisis.

In light of that, Republicans in this committee are taking extra precaution to consider all the causes of this crisis and produce a comprehensive solution to a very complex problem. Some on the other side of this dais would have us believe that the solution to the crisis is simply providing the Puerto Rican government tools to restructure their enormous debt by using Chapter 9 of the Bankruptcy Code. I would remind everyone here that Chapter 9 is a process, not a solution.

Furthermore, the claim that the island's miseries will be washed away by extending their government the use of Chapter 9, I believe is shortsighted and naïve to say the least. What we are able to determine, despite the lack of access to accurate financial audits from the government of Puerto Rico, is that cramming down debt at this stage will only hurt the problems concerning their current liquidity and access to the financial markets.

But the real detriment of offering shortsighted solutions would ignore the real cause of the problem steeped in poor budgeting standards, over-bloated government agencies, lack of fiscal transparency and accountability, and severe lack of credibility on the municipal bond market. The key root causes of the economic crisis, coupled with astronomical debt, are producing further deterioration of essential services being provided to the populace.

In order for the island to begin to truly recover from this dire situation, there need to be actual reforms within the island. The Americans living in Puerto Rico—these are all Americans—are demanding strong leadership, capable of making the necessary structural reforms and the hard choices, to get the economy growing again and employment opportunities back. These are nothing less than the benefits that come with living within the United States, namely accountability in government, responsibility in fiscal management, and opportunities to create, innovate, and thrive within a tolerable business climate, a climate where energy prices are manageable and regulations do not hinder the ability for economic growth.

If Puerto Rico is incapable or unwilling to provide these opportunities for these Americans, then the Federal Government has a responsibility to assist the island and help provide these opportunities that are lacking and desperately needed. To quote Speaker Ryan, who put it so eloquently in his address last December, "What government is supposed to do is create an environment where the individual can thrive and communities can bloom. In other words, government makes things possible, but the people make them happen." Americans calling the territory home deserve nothing less.

The opportunity to recover from this crisis with strong leadership and assistance from the Federal Government is the end solution we here in this committee are aiming to provide. We would hope our colleagues on the other side of the aisle heed our call for developing a real, comprehensive, and meaningful solution to present the President.

We want to put Puerto Rico on a sustainable path toward full-term recovery and see this island thrive and prosper for the next 100 years and beyond. I would say one thing on my behalf, had we done what I wanted to do 15 years ago, we would not be in this mess. If we had made Puerto Rico a state, which they wanted to do, but Congress did not act. I will always blame Congress for that. This is a territory that should be a state, and I have been very partisan of that, not Republican or Democrat, but because I believe in it.

I also suggest respectfully that this is a very difficult time for me because I am very strong on Puerto Rico and we do have a financial crisis. We are here today to try to solve that crisis. We would like to find out from the witnesses what they would suggest, and in doing so maybe we can have these Americans, who have put their lives on the line every day like every other American, be recognized. We have neglected for over 100 years a territory that should be a state. We have neglected main America and this Congress. And I will say shame on us. With that, I recognize the Minority Member.

[The prepared statement of Mr. Young follows:]

PREPARED STATEMENT OF THE HON. DON YOUNG, CHAIRMAN, SUBCOMMITTEE ON INDIAN, INSULAR AND ALASKA NATIVE AFFAIRS

The Subcommittee on Indian, Insular and Alaska Native Affairs meets today for an oversight hearing on, "The Need for the Establishment of a Puerto Rico Financial Stability and Economic Growth Authority."

A crisis has gripped the island of Puerto Rico. The Obama administration, Congressional Democrats, the Governor of Puerto Rico, their local territorial legislature, they are all correct, it is a crisis. And in light of that, Republicans on this committee are taking extra precaution to consider all the causes of this crisis and produce a comprehensive solution to a very complex problem.

Some on the other side of this dais would have you believe that the solution to the crisis is simply providing Puerto Rico's government tools to restructure their enormous debt using Chapter 9 of the bankruptcy code. I would remind everyone here that Chapter 9 is a process, not a solution. Furthermore, to claim that the island's miseries will be washed away by extending their government the use of Chapter 9 is shortsighted and naïve, to say the least. What we are able to determine, despite the lack of access to accurate financial audits from the government of Puerto Rico, is that cramming down debt at this stage will only exacerbate the problems concerning their current liquidity and access to the financial markets. But the real detriment of offering shortsighted solutions would be to ignore the real causes of the problem steeped in poor budgeting standards, over bloated government agencies, lack of fiscal transparency and accountability, and severe lack of credibility on the municipal bond markets. These key root causes of the economic crisis, coupled with the astronomical debt, are producing further deterioration of essential services being provided to the populace.

In order for the island to begin to truly recover from this dire situation, there needs to be actual reforms within the island. The Americans living in Puerto Rico are demanding strong leadership, capable of making the necessary structural reforms, the hard choices, to get the economy growing again and the employment opportunities back. They deserve nothing less than the benefits that come with living within the United States, namely accountability in government, responsibility in fiscal management, and opportunities to create, innovate, and thrive within a tolerable business climate. A climate where energy prices are manageable and regulations do not hinder ability for economic growth. If Puerto Rico is incapable or unwilling to provide these opportunities for those Americans, then the Federal Government has a responsibility to assist the island and help provide those opportunities that are lacking and so desperately needed. To quote Speaker Ryan, who put it so eloquently in his address last December, "What government is supposed to do is create an environment where the individual can thrive and communities can bloom. In other words, government makes things possible, but the people make them happen." Americans calling the territory home deserve nothing less.

The opportunity to recover from this crisis, with strong leadership and assistance from the Federal Government, is the end solution we here on this committee are aiming to provide. We would hope our colleagues on the other side of the aisle heed our call for developing a real, comprehensive, meaningful solution to present the President. Republicans here in Congress are not interested in a quick, meaningless short-term fix. We want to put Puerto Rico on a sustainable path toward full long-term recovery and see that island thrive and prosper for the next 100 years and beyond.

———

STATEMENT OF THE HON. PEDRO R. PIERLUISI, RESIDENT COMMISSIONER FOR THE COMMONWEALTH OF PUERTO RICO

Mr. PIERLUISI. Thank you, Chairman Young. Following this hearing, the Natural Resources Committee will craft legislation on Puerto Rico. To become law, the bill must be bipartisan and balanced. That means we are either going to pass a good bill or no bill at all.

If no bill is enacted, the already grave situation in Puerto Rico will get worse. That would not be in the national interest, in the interest of my constituents, or in the interest of Puerto Rico's creditors, many of whom are also my constituents. The drafting process should be informed by two bills that Congress enacted for Washington, DC in 1995 and 1997, which are best viewed as a single legislative package.

Washington, DC and Puerto Rico are different in material respects, so the DC package should guide, but not dictate, the Puerto Rico bill. The legislation should be holistic, containing three elements.

First, the Puerto Rico government has a record of fiscal mismanagement. We must acknowledge this painful fact, vow to do better for our constituents, and accept some temporary assistance along the way. As I have previously stated, I would support the creation of an independent board to approve the Puerto Rico government's financial plan and annual budgets, to confirm that the Puerto Rico government adheres to both throughout the fiscal year, and to ensure the publication of accurate and timely financial information.

A board can serve as a bridge to a brighter future, enabling the Puerto Rico government to perform more effectively and regain access to the financial markets. The DC oversight board was successful in instilling fiscal discipline only because it had buy-in from local government, business, and labor leaders. To achieve similar support, the Puerto Rico board must be carefully calibrated. As a territory, Puerto Rico has no democracy at the national level. If a bill seeks to extinguish our democracy at the local level, I will do everything in my power to defeat it.

Second, the Puerto Rico government must restructure its bonded debt. I say this with regret. Individuals and institutions loaned Puerto Rico money, and Puerto Rico promised to pay them back with interest. So, you will never hear me vilify creditors.

However, while bond-issuing entities in Puerto Rico can pay some of their debts, they cannot pay all of their debts under the current terms and conditions, without compromising quality of life and economic growth in the territory to an unacceptable degree. This assertion should not be subject to reasonable dispute.

Unlike the states, Puerto Rico has no authority under Federal law to restructure debt. There is a consensus among objective observers that Congress should grant Puerto Rico such authority, which would cost taxpayers nothing. I would be open to a provision that requires the oversight board to appoint a neutral third party to mediate consensual debt restructuring negotiations between bond issuing entities in Puerto Rico and their creditors, in order to reach agreements that restructure Puerto Rico's debt to a sustainable level, provide fair treatment to creditors, and can be confirmed and enforced by a Federal court. When it comes to restructuring authority, I will be flexible regarding the means to the end, but not the end itself.

Finally, the legislation should provide Puerto Rico with more state-like treatment under Federal programs, because decades of neglect from Washington is the root cause of the territory's economic, fiscal, and migration problems. I join Chairman Young's statement. Puerto Rico should have been treated equally a long time ago. A long time ago, Puerto Rico should have joined this union.

So, when we ask for state-like treatment, this is not charity or a bailout; this is about fundamental justice. If Puerto Rico were a state, the problems we confront today would not exist, or at least not in such severe form. Puerto Rico would have voting representatives in Congress to defend its interests, parity under all Federal programs, and access to Chapter 9 of the Federal Bankruptcy Code. Island leaders would not have to come hat in hand, imploring Congress to grant Puerto Rico rights and powers that every state takes for granted.

More equitable treatment is consistent with precedent. The legislative package for Washington, DC has provided the capital city with billions of dollars in funding and savings. The forthcoming bill cannot eliminate every inequality Puerto Rico faces, because only statehood could accomplish that, but it should make a real effort to mitigate certain disparities.

Let me close with an appeal to my colleagues. Before you try to come up with all sorts of clever and convoluted ways to respond to the crisis in Puerto Rico, you should simply extend to the territory those Federal programs and policies that have already proven effective in the states that you represent. Resist the urge to experiment with my constituents' lives. Equality is the best policy.

Thank you, Chairman.

[The prepared statement of Mr. Pierluisi follows:]

PREPARED STATEMENT OF THE HON. PEDRO R. PIERLUISI, RESIDENT COMMISSIONER OF PUERTO RICO

Thank you, Chairman Young. Following this hearing, the Natural Resources Committee will spearhead an effort to craft legislation on Puerto Rico.

To become law, the bill must be bipartisan and balanced. A bad bill will not be approved by both chambers of Congress and signed into law by the President. So, we are either going to pass a good bill or no bill at all.

If no bill is enacted, the already-grave situation in Puerto Rico, a U.S. territory home to 3.5 million Americans, will get worse. That would not be in the national interest, in the interest of my constituents, or in the interest of Puerto Rico's creditors, many of whom are *also* my constituents. Therefore, this Congress should act swiftly and wisely.

The drafting process should be informed by two bills that Congress enacted for Washington, DC in the 1990s—the District of Columbia Financial Responsibility and Management Assistance Act of 1995 and the National Capital Revitalization and Self-Government Improvement Act of 1997, which are best viewed as a single legislative package. However, Washington, DC and Puerto Rico are different in material respects, so the DC package should guide—but not dictate—the contents of the Puerto Rico bill.

To actually address the problem, the legislation must be holistic, containing three essential elements.

First, the Puerto Rico government has a record of fiscal mismanagement. We must acknowledge this painful fact, vow to do better for our constituents, and accept some temporary assistance along the way. Accordingly, I would support the creation of an independent board to approve the Puerto Rico government's long-term financial plan and annual budgets, to help ensure that the Puerto Rico government adheres to both throughout the fiscal year, and to make certain that the Puerto Rico government publishes accurate and timely financial information. A good board can serve as a bridge to a brighter future, helping the Puerto Rico government to perform more effectively and to regain access to the credit markets. As Mayor Williams can attest, the DC oversight board—which was active for 5 years—was successful in instilling fiscal discipline only because it had "buy-in" from the DC government, business leaders, and labor leaders. To achieve similar support, the Puerto Rico board must be carefully calibrated. As a territory, Puerto Rico has no democracy at the national level. If the forthcoming bill seeks to extinguish rather than enhance our democracy at the local level, I will do everything within my power to defeat it.

Second, the Puerto Rico government must restructure its bonded debt. I say this with genuine regret. Individuals and institutions loaned Puerto Rico money, and Puerto Rico promised to pay them back with interest. So, you will never hear me vilify creditors. But the reality is that, while bond-issuing entities in Puerto Rico can pay some of this debt, they cannot pay all of this debt, based on its current terms and conditions, without compromising quality of life and economic growth in the territory to an unacceptable degree. I don't believe this assertion is subject to reasonable dispute.

Unlike the states, Puerto Rico has no authority under Federal law to restructure any of its debt. There is a virtual consensus among objective observers that Congress should grant Puerto Rico such authority, a measure that would cost the Federal Government and U.S. taxpayers nothing. As Mr. Spiotto demonstrates in his written testimony, there are different debt restructuring models that Congress can adopt for the territory. For example, I would be open to a provision that requires the oversight board to appoint a neutral third-party to mediate consensual debt restructuring negotiations between bond-issuing entities in Puerto Rico and their creditors in order to reach agreements that (1) restructure Puerto Rico's outstanding debt so that it is sustainable, (2) provide creditors with fair and appropriate treatment, and (3) can be confirmed and enforced by a Federal court. In short, when it comes to debt adjustment, I will be flexible regarding the means to the end, but not regarding the end itself.

Finally, the legislation should provide Puerto Rico with more equitable—that is, more state-like—treatment under Federal spending and tax credit programs, because decades of neglect from Washington is the single greatest cause of the territory's economic, fiscal and migration problems. This is the furthest thing from charity or a "bailout." This is about fundamental justice. The reality is that, if Puerto Rico were a state, the problems that the island confronts today would not exist, or at least would not exist in such severe form. As a state, Puerto Rico would have seven voting representatives in Congress to defend its interests, Puerto Rico would have parity under all Federal programs, and Puerto Rico would have access to Chapter 9 of the Federal bankruptcy code. Island leaders would not have to come, hat in hand, imploring this Congress to grant Puerto Rico rights and powers that every state takes for granted.

More equitable treatment for Puerto Rico is fully consistent with precedent. The legislative package for Washington, DC—in particular, the 1997 Revitalization Act—has injected billions of dollars into the capital city and reduced the DC government's financial burden by billions of dollars as well. I recognize that the forthcoming bill cannot eliminate all of the disparities that Puerto Rico faces—because only statehood can accomplish that—but the legislation should make a meaningful effort to mitigate some of the key disparities.

Let me close with an appeal to my colleagues from both parties. Before you try to come up with all sorts of clever and convoluted ways to respond to the crisis in Puerto Rico, you should simply extend to the territory those Federal programs and policies that have already proven effective in the states that *you* represent. This is not the time to experiment; equality is the best policy.

Thank you.

Mr. YOUNG. Thank you for a very good statement, echoing my thoughts. You are a smart member of this committee.

We will start with Mr. Mayor.

And welcome, by the way, Mr. Mayor. I thought you were a great mayor. I don't know what your constituents thought, but I thought you were, so you may proceed. I am a little bit lenient, but I try to keep to the 5 minutes. If you are being very eloquent, I will let you extend it a little bit, as the rest of the members of this committee do, but it is usually 5 minutes. You watch that little thing, and it will tell you what to do.

Mr. Mayor, you are up, Mr. Williams.

STATEMENT OF THE HON. ANTHONY A. WILLIAMS, SENIOR ADVISOR, DENTONS US LLP; AND FORMER MAYOR OF WASHINGTON, DC

Mr. WILLIAMS. Well, first of all, Mr. Chairman, thank you for your generosity and your kind comments. And on that note, I probably should leave, but I will also thank the members of the subcommittee for inviting me today to testify on this important matter.

I want to highlight just a few central points in my written testimony and be as brief as possible in deference to the other speakers and the members of the committee. I benefit from my experience today talking to you as CFO of a congressionally created entity that oversaw the fiscal recovery of our Nation's capital.

Recognizing that every situation is different, I believe the time has come to explore the creation by Congress of an entity that can facilitate returning Puerto Rico to a position of sustained financial stability to create, as the speaker would say, an environment of success that induces investment.

For the reasons I will address, I support the creation of such an entity with authorities and responsibilities that would aid and empower the Commonwealth to realize fiscal stability and economic growth. Let me start by initially observing that any solution to Puerto Rico's fiscal challenges requires that this entity, which the subcommittee is considering, be created to give focused attention to how best to resolve the island's myriad expected and substantial bond defaults.

Unquestionably, the extent of impending defaults and the seemingly increasing inability of the Commonwealth to meet these obligations warrants an independent entity to be put in a position to help find a workable and fair solution acceptable not only to the people of Puerto Rico, but also to the creditors. And these are not only the bondholders, but other creditors in terms of pensioners who are owed over $70 billion.

The fact that these problems have been the subject of considerable and increasing focus for more than 2 years, with no real signs that the various constituencies are coming to common ground, to me further underscores a need for a fresh and independent team of neutrals with expertise in addressing governmental financial distress to be empaneled to both help develop sustainable solutions and to forge trust and build cooperation among the competing factions.

But let me be clear, I do not take sides about whether any such bondholder concessions are really needed, or how much, or for that matter who, other than bondholders, might also be expected to participate in making concessions to bring budgets into balance now and into the foreseeable future. Indeed, until the entity we suggest undertakes much of what will be tasked, the extent of any required concessions cannot be known. When you have a series of unaudited opinions, when you have a situation of great financial uncertainty, I think it makes sense to get the financial house in order, get financial reporting in order, get a dashboard in place before decisions can be made.

Hence, what I believe is simply that an independent group of financial sophisticated people, who collectively bring a combination of government efficiency and financial distress expertise, can play a critical and disciplined role in first developing a set of financial and operating strategies, and then hopefully by achieving consensus among disparate constituencies, implement these strategies to ensure that the Puerto Rican government will be fiscally sound and the island's economy once again is growing and vibrant.

Turning again to the wisdom of tasking the contemplated entity with the additional goal of fostering the island's economic growth, I don't think anyone can take issue with the view that it would be most desirable if Puerto Rico could increase its tax base through new inbound investments by mainland companies and plants in island operations, thereby producing new taxable income and expanding the workforce. Utilizing that approach to achieving revenue improvement would be a far preferable means to ameliorate the distress we are talking about then simply cramming down debt or cramming down liabilities to any creditor.

To provide the most optimistic environment for growing Puerto Rico's economy, it is essential that the Commonwealth be seen as fulfilling as much of its debt obligations as possible, and that is why I am so pleased that the committee has recognized that one of the key functions of the contemplated authority should be to look at tangible ways for the island, to the fullest extent possible, grow out of its debt problems through stimulated economic expansion and increased tax revenues.

In my view, this committee's focus on economic expansion can also demonstrate to the people the commitment of Congress to assist the island in achieving long-term financial stability predicated not only on finding efficiencies in delivery of their government services, but at least equally so on the healthier and growing economy that fosters new, well-paying, private sector jobs.

Hearkening further to my DC experience, the subcommittee's apparent legislative approach appears quite similar to the motivation behind creating an independent authority for Washington, namely to provide meaningful guidance to all affected constituencies to help develop and fashion innovative approaches and to foster cooperation among all affected constituencies. Like the DC approach, the focus of this entity should certainly be forward-looking, and not to point blame on anyone in who shot John and all that, but forward-looking, solving the problem, enacting a vision based on the input from all the different parties.

The problems presented by Puerto Rico's current financial challenges are complex. The goal of Congress, if it pursues the authority's creation, should be to provide Puerto Rico with the best means available to help remedy the fiscal distress as soon as possible, and in so doing to deliver the kind of economic expansion and settled expectations that I am talking about.

Since my time is rapidly dwindling away, I want to focus on several additional key points regarding my views about the structure of this entity.

One, I believe that Congress should keep the composition of the authority to a limited number. I think five and no more than seven members would achieve the right balance.

Two, I strongly advocate that the authority appoint a CFO or a financial executive to be involved in the coordination of the authority's activities, and also to work day to day with the Commonwealth's administration and its legislature to create reliable budgets and long-term financial plans, to work with the government of Puerto Rico on creating reliable revenue estimates and expenditure forecasts, and to give this entity, based on that cooperation and sometimes notwithstanding that cooperation, the approval authority over these budgets and financial plans.

Likewise, Congress should ensure that the authorities and members will be prepared to commit to a significant and sustained workload for a considerable period. It will also need to retain a staff of financial and legal professionals to work at their direction in both conceiving and effectuating various initiatives.

As I said, the financial condition presented today is very complex, there are an array of challenges, and I think nothing short of a fully committed effort can be expected to accomplish what Congress envisions.

Next——

Mr. YOUNG. Mr. Mayor, you are 2 minutes and 35——

Mr. WILLIAMS. OK.

Mr. YOUNG. I was a little bit—you are close?

Mr. WILLIAMS. One final thing. The power and authority that Congress vests in the authority needs to be sufficient to get the job done, once and for all. While, in the District there were two Acts that the Ranking Member recollects were part of our recovery, as much as possible if the work can all be done at one time, I think we will be that much further down the road to creating the kind of environment of success, the settled expectations that will begin to bring back the investment to the island, and create the kind of economic recovery that we are all seeking for the people there.

Thank you, sir.

[The prepared statement of Mr. Williams follows:]

PREPARED STATEMENT OF ANTHONY A. WILLIAMS, SENIOR STRATEGIC ADVISOR TO DENTONS U.S. LLP, FORMER MAYOR OF WASHINGTON, DC

As the former CFO of Washington, DC, appointed by the congressionally established financial control board for the District, working at the direction of both, and having subsequently served for two terms as the Mayor of our Nation's Capital, I appreciate the opportunity to share my views with the subcommittee regarding the significant merits for creating an authority for what the subcommittee has noticed for hearing.

The people of Puerto Rico are entitled to a prosperous and sustainable economic future. Taking the necessary steps to assist the Commonwealth in timely implementing solutions to its well-recognized financial challenges is important not only to the Island but to the Nation as a whole; and I believe that the legislative actions being considered by this subcommittee, as well as other legislative initiatives that are the province of yet other House committees, hopefully with bipartisan support, can provide the impetus and foundation for returning the Island to a position of fiscal strength and a pathway to its economic independence.

Puerto Rico is not alone in having to address serious financial distress. For various reasons often unique to each locale, and despite best intentions, such financial challenges have arisen in other highly respected communities that today are financially successful. In addition to Washington, DC which when I assumed its reins as CFO was facing deep and persistent fiscal challenges, several of our other major cities—notably, New York, Philadelphia and Cleveland—each also benefited from having a financial control board assist them in emerging from deep financial distress and foster their successful and sustained economic recoveries.

Before providing some focused observations regarding the scope of responsibilities of the Federal Authority which this subcommittee is considering, as well as other important aspects that are critical to its success, I wish to speak to the concerns that will unquestionably surface, just as they did when Congress created a Federal board to assume responsibility for DC's distressed fiscal affairs. Naturally, the assertion will be made that permitting another government to provide some assistance and leadership denies the populace their voice in self-determination. But while it is easy to adopt that rhetoric, our history and my personal experience as Washington's CFO, teaches that whatever negative hue and cry is initially heard, readily erodes as positive developments achieved by a neutral body start taking hold. This was the case with the independent financial board created for DC, as well as with the Metropolitan Assistance Corporation created for NY in the 1970s; and has proved true more recently when state fiscal responsibility for the cities of Detroit and Pennsylvania's capital city, Harrisburg, were reposed in state-appointed managers. In each of these situations, the residents, community leaders, civic organizations and business interests came to accept and indeed support the expertise and fresh perspective offered by the independent neutrals; and I firmly believe that such will be the case if Congress were to take similar action to meaningfully bolster Puerto Rico's prospect for prosperity and fiscal independence.

Rather than independent leadership being seen in hindsight as troublesome, all these situations illustrate that creating something new, fresh with ideas, and not wedded to the notions of any particular constituency, can help build the belief in a bright and vibrant future for a financially troubled government and provide the path by which once divergent interests can come to a consensual understanding. Viewed from real examples of success and not premised on fears of divisiveness, congressional action to create legislation for the type of authority that is contemplated by this subcommittee is properly perceived as the optimal means, as expeditiously as possible, to resolve the Commonwealth's current financial difficulties. Perhaps more importantly, this congressional effort can be accepted as the start of real and meaningful solutions to grow the Commonwealth's economy, create private sector jobs and encourage many who have left the Island to return, ultimately making the people of Puerto Rico secure and proud.

In my view, the time is now for Congress to create an authority that would have as its goals both achieving financial stability and a balanced budget for the Island, while also focusing on economic growth strategies that over time can assist the Island in gaining true financial independence.

Regarding the need for a Federal Government Authority to provide fiscal stability leadership, both the current inability of the GDB and the Island's administration to solve imminent defaults, as well as the sheer magnitude of the debt liabilities, alone justify congressional action. Especially this is so when we also factor in the number of distinct bond issues that are expected to suffer defaults, the fact that the Puerto Rican administration very recently predicted even greater current budget shortfalls than what it saw as the case only a few months earlier and, significantly, the recognition that apart from impending bond defaults, there looms both quickly growing unfunded healthcare costs as well as an enormous underfunded public employee pension liability that some have estimated to be in the $50 billion range.

Additionally, with $72 billion in Puerto Rican bond obligations at stake, Congress needs to be mindful of the consequences to the cost of municipal credit across our Nation if the Island's debt obligations are not resolved in a manner that the municipal bond market sees as fair and equitable. Our states and cities have for well over a century benefited from the low cost of credit extended by the bond market to fund essential capital expenses; and with our aging infrastructure and widespread concerns over the level of pension underfunding—exacerbated by recent turmoil in the equity markets—the need for the continuation of relatively low cost of credit for our states and cities cannot be overstated. In this context, Puerto Rico's fiscal challenges and their resolution are the Nation's concern since anything less than a balanced and fair solution to Puerto Rico's debt problems runs the real risk of driving up the cost of credit for our cities and states just at a time when they will need to borrow more.

I recognize and acknowledge that the Puerto Rican government has been expending significant efforts to develop workable solutions to the Island's serious fiscal challenges, and that it has devoted focused attention to this process in earnest for the past 2 years. But the time and effort that has been devoted to date, with the lack of any clear comprehensive set of solutions at present, certainly merit pursuit of a new and different approach and underscores the need for a federally created authority composed of independent professionals to help fashion a resolution that all constituencies can come to perceive as both sustainable and balanced.

I am most pleased that this subcommittee is not only focusing on creating an authority designed to solve the current budgetary shortfalls, but has also recognized that economic growth for Puerto Rico is key to the Island's future. Maximizing the extent to which budget shortfalls can be meaningfully narrowed over time through real growth in the Island's tax base is certainly preferable to relying on concessions from creditors, be they bondholders, the government's current labor force or public employee retirees, as the only means to bring current and future budgets into balance. Growing Puerto Rico's way out of its fiscal distress over time by relying on the revenues derived from an increase of its tax base is not only the most honorable path; excitement about the Commonwealth's economic resurgence can build on itself and make the Island a vibrant and attractive environment fostering fresh investments which, in turn, can create new well-paying jobs, reverse the recent trend of out-migration and bring back many who left the Island in search of opportunities.

Believing that economic growth is one of several key components that can help address the Island's current fiscal distress I must be candid to observe that I do not believe that the authority which this subcommittee contemplates creating can alone provide the means to attract new in-bound investment in the Island's economy. Unquestionably, solving the Island's fiscal instability and looming government defaults is essential, because the current environment is certainly not conducive to attracting substantial investments. But solving the immediate fiscal crisis, while absolutely essential, will not alone be sufficient to bring the Island back to the position of economic self-sufficiency that it enjoyed as recently as a decade ago. Other congressional legislation is needed.

Costs of production in Puerto Rico, not unlike other island economies, are significantly higher than on the Mainland; and without here belaboring the various causes of such incremental production and related transportation costs, resulting in them being meaningfully higher than similar Mainland production, in my opinion some form of favorable tax-based incentives need to be offered to businesses willing to locate operations on the Island to offset these higher production and transportation costs. Such tax incentive measures that were previously adopted by Congress worked to attract significant investment in the Commonwealth's economy; and taking those incentives away, as occurred in 2006, in hindsight has proven ill-advised. While another committee of the House, acting in concert with this subcommittee, will have to assess the merits of adopting carefully considered new tax incentive measures and their details, I believe that such legislation is essential if the authority contemplated by this subcommittee to oversee the Island's return to financial stability and economic independence is to be afforded the tools that will allow it, acting in close cooperation with the Commonwealth's economic growth professionals, to significantly attract meaningful in-bound investment. If so, there can be real hope that over time such investments can produce the level of tax-base growth that can play a meaningful role in reducing Puerto Rico's budgetary imbalances and serve as a key component in Puerto Rico's fiscal recovery and financial self-sufficiency.

Having addressed the overarching considerations that I believe merit the wisdom behind creating the kind of authority that this subcommittee is currently considering, let me complete my testimony by offering some general observations regarding the duties of such an authority, its duration and the composition of its membership.

Starting with its duties, and without attempting here to set forth every component of the authority's powers, responsibilities and obligations, let me first briefly observe what I see as the prudent steps that the authority will wish to undertake to accomplish its congressionally established mandates. An essential first step is developing an agreed set of realistic and current financial data regarding the revenues and expenses of each unit of government experiencing budgetary challenges. Despite the best of intentions, the current environment is such that neither Congress nor any of its creditor constituencies have confidence in the existing and promulgated data; and, whether that lack of confidence is accurate or misperceived, it is critical that all constituencies come to agreement on an agreed set of financials. Clearly, the authority will play a vital role in assuring that all the data is transparent and that all constituencies can have confidence in the data that will be used to formulate appropriate courses of action.

With an accurate handle on all current revenue sources, debts and operating expenses, the authority will then turn its intention to two immediate and challenging tasks; first, to explore all possible means to raise or collect additional tax or fee revenues and reduce operating costs; and second, short of developing a comprehensive fiscal recovery plan that will require considerable time to fashion and then negotiate, determine how best to address the near term anticipated financial defaults, while longer range solutions that can maximize the repayment of what Puerto Rico has borrowed are fully explored. Make no mistake, these initial tasks are formidable; and Congress ought to vest the authority with an array of powers that will permit it to do its work and that will both foster the willingness of all affected parties to actively participate in designing and implementing the optimal means to achieve sustainable increases in revenues and reductions in operating costs, and, at the same time, permit the authority to implement with bond creditor cooperation fair interim solutions that address anticipated bond payment defaults, thereby avoiding what most would consider non-productive related litigation.

As all potential incremental revenue sources are explored, the authority ought to determine what currently non-utilized public capital assets are available, and the possible means to monetize those assets through joint ventures with private market investors. Such monetizations ought to be designed to provide the Puerto Rican government over time with additional cash-flows that can be used to help narrow budget shortfalls. Moreover, such joint ventures should be in interim solutions to the bond payment defaults structured to provide the Puerto Rican government with additional upsides based on contractual mechanisms that permit it to share in the increased value of such monetized assets as its economy recovers and expands.

In assessing new revenue that can be a source of funding future budgets, the authority will also want to develop realistic projections regarding the broadened tax base that can be achieved through tax-incentivized in-bound investment. This will require significant tangible proof regarding the extent and timing of additional revenues that these economic incentives once put in place can generate; and the financial markets, the Puerto Rican government and the credit rating agencies will all need to come to a consensus about these projections based on actual commitments from leading Mainland companies to invest on the Island.

Ultimately, after the authority works with the cooperation of both the Puerto Rican government and all affected parties to implement every available means to increase revenues and reduce the operating expenses of each of the government units, it will become necessary to assess whether and to what extent, net of such revenue improvements and operating expense reductions, some budget shortfalls may still exist, factoring into the analysis both future underfunded pension liabilities and unfunded and rising healthcare obligations. Here again, we must be realistic and recognize that despite best efforts, some concessions may well be required. In such event, likely the most challenging aspect of the authority's work will be to address how to fairly and equitably allocate the need for some concessions among all constituencies. If that is the case, ideally, the authority can foster an atmosphere where required concessions can be consensually negotiated; and here again Congress ought to provide the authority with a variety of tools that both foster the authority's ability to enhance the prospect of consent and that afford it the flexibility to address complex issues. In the final analysis, all affected parties will hopefully see the virtues of negotiating an agreed, and therefore certain, resolution as far preferable to the cost and delays associated with protracted and uncertain litigation if the authority were to be forced to exercise available remedies to compel concessions.

In the final analysis, the extensive work that will be required, the complexity of the issues presented, the need to harmonize divergent views about what is fair and the breadth of assignments that the authority will be required to undertake as it pursues a sustainable and comprehensive resolution of Puerto Rico's financial recovery are formidable. Unquestionably, tasking the authority with these challenges is a tall order. But, in my opinion, anything less robust than the work of such an authority is not going to provide a sustainable solution to Puerto Rico's serious financial challenges; and waiting any longer to see if somehow the situation self corrects is fundamentally misguided.

Regarding the period of time that the authority might need to be kept in place, much depends on the time needed to successfully solve the budget deficits and the growth of the Puerto Rican economy. It is premature to know now when the role of the authority can be terminated or under what circumstances its functions and oversights can be narrowed. Unquestionably, if part of the debt solution will require the time for repayment of borrowings to be extended, bondholders are going to require that the authority monitor actual performance to the pro forma projections, and have the ability to fashion revised solutions if, despite best intentions, the established benchmarks are not being met. This kind of residual right to monitor and adjust actions, key to other similar control authorities, even if never utilized, provides the kind of comfort that creditors will justifiably demand and is fundamental to constituencies agreeing to the restructuring of Puerto Rico's financial obligations.

Finally, permit me to comment on the composition of the authority. Naturally, the starting point is to ensure that its members possess the hands-on experience and/ or professional training that brings sophistication, experience and expertise to address Puerto Rico's financial distress. The size of the authority's membership should be sufficient to allow for different perspectives and diverse backgrounds, but not so unwieldy as to make the very active work of the authority unmanageable. Perhaps five, but not more than seven, members would seem to balance these competing considerations.

In my view, it is essential to have some of the membership of the authority be comprised of people who can offer the Puerto Rican perspective. While it is vitally important that all of the members be independent, and not perceived as having a conflict by reason of being part of the government of Puerto Rico or a creditor thereof, I think it is critically important to the process that Congress assure that some portion of the authority's membership be selected either from Puerto Rican residents or from those who have lived and worked for some time in and are of Puerto Rican ancestry. Having in-depth experience with Puerto Rico's economy is yet another attribute that also ought to be considered in selecting membership on the authority. Importantly, too, Congress ought to look to members that well understand the workings of the financial markets.

Realistically, the authority's members will need to be prepared to devote significant time every week to meetings or conferences, especially so in the beginning several months; and members ought to be vetted to confirm their willingness to devote substantial energies to the authority's work. Certainly, the authority will require and rely upon a staff of financial and legal professionals that can provide advice to the members but, as importantly, also undertake or work on a variety of tasks at the direction of the authority's members. I also see considerable wisdom in the members selecting a CFO to coordinate the staff, but also actively interface regularly with the Puerto Rican administration on numerous matters while also frequently meeting with various creditor constituencies. Perhaps other duties will require additional appointments such as an information officer; but the members can consider these additional appointments as the circumstances may appear to warrant.

In conclusion, I sincerely appreciate the opportunity this subcommittee has afforded me to address the important fiscal challenges that the Commonwealth of Puerto Rico is facing. Paramount in my view is securing a bright economic future for the people of Puerto Rico; and I hope my views are seen as motivated by that goal.

Mr. YOUNG. Thank you for a great testimony.

Mr. Carlos Garcia.

STATEMENT OF CARLOS M. GARCIA, CHIEF EXECUTIVE OFFICER, BAYBOSTON MANAGERS, LLC AND FORMER CHAIRMAN AND PRESIDENT OF THE GOVERNMENT DEVELOPMENT BANK OF PUERTO RICO, NEWTON CENTRE, MASSACHUSETTS

Mr. GARCIA. Good morning, Chairman Young, Resident Commissioner Pierluisi, other distinguished members of this committee, and all that have an interest of Puerto Rico. My name is Carlos Garcia. I was the chairman, president, and CEO of the Government Development Bank for Puerto Rico from January 2009 to March 2011.

In addition, I was appointed as chairman of the Puerto Rico Fiscal Restructuring and Stabilization Board, a local fiscal control board created by law in March of 2009 with a comprehensive and joint mandate to address a complex fiscal emergency created through many years of fiscal imbalances and, in my opinion, the negative tail economic effect of the decision to repeal Section 936, which provided a manufacturing center for the world in Puerto Rico and was aggravated by Puerto Rico's failure to develop an alternative economic plan.

The second task was to ensure the continuation of essential services to the people of Puerto Rico and to safeguard Puerto Rico's credit rating. The local control board acted swiftly by creating and executing a fiscal stabilization plan. It executed this plan with transparency to all Puerto Rico stakeholders, including a creation of a funded program to mitigate the socio-economic effects of its mandate.

It was a very difficult and unpopular job, not void of controversy; but by 2011, the swift actions of the local board, the Governor of Puerto Rico, the legislature and its cabinet provided a fiscal stabilization, including a double-digit reduction in government expenses, 2 straight years of surpassed government budgeted revenues, the timely delivery of financial statements, and an unparalleled reduction of the fiscal deficit.

It re-established the access to the municipal market and also the first credit rating upgrades and the highest investment grade credit ratings in almost three decades, and started the beginning of an economic stabilization. The local control board was composed of a team of five cabinet-level officials with ministerial responsibilities over fiscal oversight, government funding, revenue expenditure, labor policy, and economic development.

The work of the control board was comprehensive and effective as documented in the local control board report to the Puerto Rico legislature, dated March 31, 2011. The control board gave Puerto Rico a centralized implementation and decisionmaking arm to self-adjust itself out of its pre-2009 fiscal crisis. It only had a 2-year mandate, which in my belief was too short. The local board did not have powers to eliminate or consolidate government agencies or to implement structural economic, labor, or tax measures, which was a shortcoming.

After the local control board disbanded in 2011, the strength of its centralized programs as well as its implementation arm disappeared. What happened after the local control board disappeared is painfully known to all of us today, as many of these things could have been averted. But the question is: How can Puerto Rico break out of this treacherous downward spiral, and what can Congress do? In my opinion, it is imperative to create a long-term fiscal and economic authority to address holistically and comprehensively all of Puerto Rico's issues—fiscal, economic, and social, once and for all, in a credible, sensible, consistent, and swift manner. At this stage, in my opinion, the probability of success is only viable with the creation of a federally mandated Puerto Rico Fiscal and Economic Authority, enacted by Congress but with strong local participation.

The authority should be provided the powers and tools to implement structural reforms of the government of Puerto Rico and its agencies; require the prior approval by the authority of all governmental budgets, additional indebtedness, capital expenditures, and employment levels; provide for a complete overhaul of Puerto Rico's accounting, budgeting, payroll, information, and other control systems, as well as its associated processes; and manage the restructuring and renegotiation process of all of Puerto Rico's obligations under a clear framework established in the authority's Federal enabling act, based on generally accepted public debt restructuring principles.

There is no one-size-fits-all solution considering that Puerto Rico has roughly 20 issuers. The challenges are further compounded by the diversity of creditors that range from sophisticated institutional investors to 'mom and pops'. The proposed framework should provide a speedy, predictable, and orderly process that protects assets, respects creditors' rights, but also recognizes that underlying all the formal debts, there are social obligations with respect to pensions, education, and health programs.

The authority, as a single point of resolution, should arguably be better equipped by the composition of its government board to balance these equities than the bankruptcy process or other courts. As well, it is critical to attend the issues of the economy of Puerto Rico by creating jobs and generating regional activity.

Attached to my testimony is a White Paper that outlines a one-time, temporary proposal that is revenue-neutral to U.S. taxpayers to jumpstart the economic recovery of Puerto Rico by permitting U.S. corporations holding funds outside of the United States to repatriate a limited amount of those funds under the requirement that at least 50 percent of those funds are invested in activities in Puerto Rico.

My last recommendation is for the U.S. Congress to immediately confirm the current financial situation and deficit of the government of Puerto Rico via the Congressional Budget Office and require the government of Puerto Rico to issue promptly independent audited financial statements and provide monthly reporting information. One cannot fix what one cannot measure or monitor. I thank you for the privilege and honor to address you today and will gladly answer any questions on my testimony.

Thank you, Mr. Chairman.

[The prepared statement of Mr. Garcia follows:]

PREPARED STATEMENT OF CARLOS GARCIA, FORMER CHAIRMAN, PRESIDENT AND CEO OF THE GOVERNMENT DEVELOPMENT BANK FOR PUERTO RICO (2009–2011); FORMER CHAIRMAN OF THE PUERTO RICO FISCAL RESTRUCTURING AND STABILIZATION BOARD (2009–2011); AND FORMER CHAIRMAN OF THE PUERTO RICO PUBLIC PRIVATE PARTNERSHIP AUTHORITY (2009–2011)

Good morning Chairman Young, Resident Commissioner Pierluisi, other distinguished members of this committee and the U.S. House of Representatives, fellow panelists, government officials, and all that have in-mind the best interests for Puerto Rico.

My name is Carlos Garcia. I was the Chairman, President and CEO of the Government Development Bank for Puerto Rico from January 2009 to March 2011. In addition, I was also appointed as Chairman of the Puerto Rico Fiscal Restructuring and Stabilization Board ("Local Control Board"), a local fiscal control board created by law on March 9, 2009, with a joint and comprehensive mandate from the executive and legislative arms of Puerto Rico, to:

1. Address a complex fiscal emergency created through many years of fiscal imbalances and, in my opinion, the negative tail economic effect of the decision in 1996 to terminate Puerto Rico's favorable Federal tax regime set up under Section 936 of the U.S. Internal Revenue Code which helped establish Puerto Rico as a manufacturing center for the world and further aggravated by

Puerto Rico's failure to develop an alternative economic plan during the 10-year phase-out of Section 936 or persuade Congress to assist with a substitute regime;

2. Ensure the continuation of essential services to the people of Puerto Rico; and
3. Safeguard Puerto Rico's credit rating.

The Local Control Board acted swiftly by creating and executing a comprehensive fiscal stabilization plan. It executed this plan with transparency to all Puerto Rico stakeholders, including a continuous, open dialog with labor and private sector leaders as well as bondholders, constant information provided to the Puerto Rico Legislature and local media, and the creation of a funded program to mitigate the socio-economic effects of the implementation of its mandate. It was a difficult and very unpopular job, not void of controversy, but by 2011 the swift actions of the Local Control Board, the Governor of Puerto Rico and its cabinet members resulted in:

1. The fiscal stabilization of Puerto Rico finances, including a double digit reduction in government expenses, two straight years of surpassed government budgeted revenue estimates, the timely delivery of audited financial statements for Fiscal Years 2010 and 2011, and an unparalleled reduction of the fiscal deficit—in 22 months Puerto Rico's deficit in comparison to the U.S. states went from the worst (#51) to the middle of the pack (#20) [1];
2. Re-establishing access to the U.S. municipal securities market and obtaining the first credit rating upgrades and the highest investment grade credit ratings in almost three decades; and
3. The economic stabilization of Puerto Rico (as evidenced by the Puerto Rico Economic Activity Index) after coordinating the framework and deployment of Federal and local stimulus funds, implementing a public private partnership program, enacting a comprehensive tax reform reducing individual and corporate income tax rates, restructuring the local banking sector in coordination with Federal authorities, and tapping into new sources of tax revenue without permanently increasing the tax burden on its citizens or on Puerto Rico's local commercial sectors.

The Local Control Board was composed of a team of five cabinet-level officials with ministerial responsibility for fiscal oversight, government funding, government revenue, government expenditures, labor policy and economic development, namely the President of the Government Development Bank (chairman), the Secretary of the Treasury, the Director of the Office of Management and Budget, the Secretary of Labor and the Secretary of Economic Development and Commerce. The Local Control Board's mandate was mostly focused on fiscal matters, although it promoted several economic initiatives and carefully calibrated fiscal measures with the input of an economic council (composed of top private sector economists). The Local Control Board's efforts also had the support of over 30 dedicated professional staff members and a large number of hired contractors with expertise on fiscal restructurings who were physically deployed throughout the principal agencies of the government of Puerto Rico.

Under a "trust but verify" approach, the Local Control Board representatives worked side by side with all impacted government agencies. The Local Control Board also created a $1 billion program to mitigate the adverse socio-economic consequences of reducing government employment by providing counseling programs via regional centers, temporary health insurance, informational fairs, and grants to promote re-training, furthering educational attainment and entrepreneurialism.

The work of the Local Control Board was comprehensive and effective as documented in the Local Control Board report to the Puerto Rico Legislature dated March 31, 2011 (the report in Spanish is attached to my testimony). The Control Board gave Puerto Rico a centralized implementation and decisionmaking arm to self-adjust itself out of its pre-2009 fiscal crisis. The Local Control Board's report provides a complete and consolidated account of all the actions taken, and it presented a comprehensive picture of Puerto Rico's overall indebtedness. The Local Control Board found almost $4 billion of unrecognized and unpaid obligations, accumulated fiscal deficits, loans without sources of repayment and other legal liabilities that had been incurred prior to 2009. All of these issues had contributed to the Puerto Rico fiscal emergency.

---

[1] Based on data from the Center on Budget and Policy Priorities and the Government Development Bank for Puerto Rico.

The Local Control Board discovered that total Puerto Rico government indebtedness in December 2008 (before the Local Control Board commenced its work) was $57.5 billion[2] and not $53.8 billion. The Local Control Board kept a tight grip on Puerto Rico's debt with a net $2.7 billion, or 5 percent, increase from December 2008 to December 2010 (versus the $33 billion or 135 percent debt increase from 2000 to 2008), and bonded-out currently payable obligations to longer maturities at a lower cost via a dedicated and segregated sales tax revenue authority called Puerto Rico Sales Tax Financing Corporation (better known for its Spanish acronym, COFINA). The aggregate amount of extra-constitutional debt obligations contracted prior to 2009 and bonded out by COFINA from 2007 to 2010 was $9.4 billion.[3]

The Local Control Board had a 2-year mandate, which I believe was too short. It had restructuring powers that were conferred by the Puerto Rico Legislature; its work was augmented by the support of the Governor of Puerto Rico and by virtue of the dual roles of its members, who were both cabinet members of the government of Puerto Rico as well as the members of the Local Control Board. Its principal powers were the ability to:

1. Design and implement a multi-year plan to achieve fiscal balance;
2. Implement legislated temporary tax revenue measures to deal with the fiscal emergency;
3. Cutback on expenditures and implement a multi-step plan to reduce the size of the government's payroll; and
4. Execute financial measures to provide the liquidity required to guaranty the essential services to the people of Puerto Rico and to fund the extra-constitutional debt (i.e. accumulated budgetary deficits, unrecognized indebtedness and unpaid bills) and a transition period to fiscal balance.

The Local Control Board's mandate was limited to Puerto Rico's central government. It did not include the Puerto Rico public corporations. The Local Control Board did not have powers to eliminate or consolidate government agencies or to implement structural economic, labor or tax measures. All of these measures were required to be presented to the Puerto Rico Legislature. The Local Control Board and its members were successful in coordinating efforts with the Puerto Rico Legislature to enact several reforms to promote economic growth or improve the fiscal situation, such as the Puerto Rico public-partnership authority, a permits reform, a tax reform, an excise tax on foreign corporations, and an energy reform. Efforts to enact a labor reform and an overhaul of the government agencies were not successful.

After the Local Control Board disbanded in 2011, the strength of its centralized budgeting, expense control, fiscal oversight and transparency reporting programs as well as its implementation arm disappeared. What happened after the Local Control Board disappeared is painfully known to all of us as we sit here today trying to find constructive solutions for a re-enacted Puerto Rico crisis that could have and should have been averted by the continued service of a control board.

I want to share with you my recommendations based on the lessons learned and the struggles confronted by acting as chairman of the only fiscal control board created in recent Puerto Rico history, in the hope that it will provide insights to this Congress to act decisively and provide Puerto Rico with the necessary tools to bring it back from its decade long recession, and for the benefit of the over 7 million Puerto Ricans that are citizens of the United States of America and represent the second largest Hispanic population in the United States.

But before I do so, please allow me the opportunity to state, in my opinion, the root cause of Puerto Rico's problems:

- The fiscal and economic troubles of Puerto Rico are due to the implementation of inconsistent local fiscal and economic policies through several decades and exacerbated by the 10-year phase out, beginning in 1996, of Puerto Rico's special fiscal tax regime, which was Section 936 of the U.S. Internal Revenue Code. Section 936 provided tax incentives for manufacturers to locate its operations in Puerto Rico, and was repealed without any substitute economic growth strategy or plan. It was Puerto Rico's main economic engine, fostering a manufacturing sector that represented 50 percent of Puerto Rico's gross do-

---

[2] See pages 11–12 of the Local Control Board report to the Puerto Rico Legislature and Annex A–4. Total Puerto Rico Government, excluding municipalities.

[3] See Annex A–6 of the Local Control Board report to the Puerto Rico Legislature for details on the use of COFINA bond proceeds.

mestic product and generated over $30 billion in low-cost funding to the local banking system that trickled down to small businesses and consumers

- This loss prompted outsized government overspending and hiring in an unsuccessful and unsustainable effort to revive the economy—mostly financed in the U.S. municipal capital markets or as part of the accumulated deficits and other debt obligations without a source of repayment (such as the ones discovered by the Local Control Board); and aggravated by inefficient public corporations and monopolies that became too complex to manage and technologically outdated. Puerto Rico therefore lost its competitive edge and the ability to generate any meaningful new economic activity.
- The end result, almost two decades after, has been the large accumulation of recurring fiscal deficits, over $70 billion in debt, and an economy incapable of generating jobs that has prompted the recent migration to the U.S. mainland of over 200,000 people who have felt that the "American Dream" is not feasible on the Island. By the time of the full phase-out of Section 936 in 2006, the Puerto Rico economy had already completely decoupled from the U.S. mainland economy, breaking with its historical trend as a regional economy that closely tracked the United States. Its initial manifestation was a local government shutdown in May 2006, which clearly marked the start of Puerto Rico's now long-lived economic downturn.
- With no special tax regime and an inefficient utilities offering, Puerto Rico quickly lost its manufacturing economic engine, and what remains today is not even a shadow of what it was, with the added threat that a significant part of the existing manufacturing production base will disappear in coming years as many of its leading products face patent protection expirations.
- Since 1996, the U.S. Government quiet response has been the continuous yearly increase of Federal transfer payments to individuals furthering the welfare state that creates a disincentive to labor force participation and providing little motivation for national and local private enterprises that cater to consumers funded from the welfare state to put capital at risk for new ventures that could generate economic activity and jobs.
- Puerto Rico is and must be accountable for its shortcomings, but nevertheless concrete action is required from this U.S. Congress to help Puerto Rico find a prosperous path again.

How can Puerto Rico break out of this treacherous, downward spiral and what can this U.S. Congress do to assist?

It is imperative to create a long-term fiscal and economic authority to address holistically and comprehensively all of Puerto Rico's issues—fiscal, economic and social, once and for all, in a credible, sensible, consistent and swift manner. The models for such an authority are the experiences learned by the city of New York in 1970s, Washington, DC in the 1990s and the Puerto Rico Control Board in 2009 to 2011.

At this stage, in my opinion, the probability of success is only viable with the creation of a federally mandated Puerto Rico Fiscal and Economic Authority ("Authority"), enacted by U.S. Congress but with strong local membership. In other words, Congress should provide the framework and the tools while qualified members of the at-large Puerto Rico community will be responsible to manage the affairs of the Authority under congressional oversight and progress reporting to the Puerto Rico Legislature.

The Authority should be composed of five members, including its chairman. The chairman should be a federally appointed, independent, full-time expert in fiscal and economic matters. The Authority should have appropriate, qualified and strong representation from the government of Puerto Rico, Puerto Rico's organized labor, Puerto Rico's private sector and Puerto Rico's civic/not-for-profit sector. Its five members should be appointed for 5-year terms after a vetting process that evaluates their qualifications and expertise to serve in this capacity. The Authority should be allocated with sufficient resources to carry out its purposes, including Federal funding to ensure its independence, and provided with technical assistance from the U.S. Treasury department and the I.R.S., among other Federal agencies, as well as designated liaisons with the White House and both chambers of U.S. Congress.

The Authority should be provided the powers and tools to:

1. Implement structural reforms of the government of Puerto Rico and its political sub-divisions (currently, over 130 agencies and public corporations and 78 municipalities) with the intent to create a more efficient and agile structure at the service of the people of Puerto Rico, which can be fully supported by

the current and recurring financial means of Puerto Rico. This will require a careful review of the essential governmental activities that should be offered by the government versus the ones that should be jointly served via public-private partnerships, privatized or terminated;

2. Require the prior approval by the Authority of all governmental budgets, additional indebtedness, capital expenditures, and employment levels;

3. Complete overhaul of Puerto Rico's accounting, budgeting, payroll, information and fiscal control systems, and its associated processes;

4. Manage the restructuring and re-negotiation process of all of Puerto Rico's obligations under a clear framework established in the Authority's Federal enabling act, based on generally accepted public debt restructuring principles, including the following powers, among others:

   a. The ability to call for a mandatory collective negotiation with all creditors;

   b. The ability to impose a stay on creditors during the negotiation process while also being able to impose provisions that protect creditors' interests during the stay period;

   c. The ability to provide liquidity to the government of Puerto Rico via direct access to a secured line of credit from the U.S. Treasury Department following similar precedents such as the Tennessee Valley Authority and Bonneville Power Administration, both created by Congressional legislation; and

   d. A provision that binds all creditors upon reaching an agreement with a majority of creditors (i.e. cramdown provision).

   There is no "one-size-fits-all" solution considering that Puerto Rico has roughly 20 issuers with different sources of revenue, debt covenants, priority of payments and bondholder rights and protections. The challenges are compounded by the diversity of creditors that range from sophisticated institutional investors to "mom and pops" who trusted their lifetime savings to the credit worthiness and promises made by the government of Puerto Rico. The proposed framework should provide a speedy, predictable and orderly process that protects assets, respects creditors' rights but also recognizes that underlying all the formal debts there are social obligations with respect to pensions, education and health programs, among others. The Authority, as a single point of resolution, should arguably be better equipped by the composition of its governing members to balance these equities than the bankruptcy process or the courts. Nevertheless, the Authority's effectiveness may be enhanced by providing access via the Authority and as a last resource to Chapter 9 bankruptcy protection for some of the most troubled Puerto Rico public corporations only;

5. Design and implement a new economic model for Puerto Rico to create jobs and generate regional economic activity throughout the Island, including recommendations for tax and labor reforms as well as a sustainable fiscal control framework.

   Attached to my testimony is a white paper that outlines a one-time, temporary proposed measure to jumpstart the economic recovery of Puerto Rico by permitting U.S. corporations holding funds outside the United States to repatriate a limited amount of those funds under the requirement that at least 50 percent of the repatriated funds be invested in activities that generate economic prosperity and jobs in Puerto Rico, in sectors such as energy, manufacturing, tourism, education, health, and rum production. This proposal should have a minimal or revenue neutral impact to U.S. taxpayers while also achieving the objective of bringing these funds into the United States;

6. Evaluate the effect of Federal policies and programs on Puerto Rico, such as Federal welfare programs, minimum wage, Medicaid, Medicare, Jones Act, etc., and provide recommendations for possible changes; and

7. Provide permanent fiscal oversight. The Authority should be a fully functional control board until Puerto Rico achieves a newfound path to prosperity as defined goals are achieved and shown to be effective. At that point, the Authority would convert to an oversight board.

My last recommendation is for U.S. Congress to immediately confirm the current financial situation and deficit of the government of Puerto Rico, working through the Congressional Budget Office, and require the government of Puerto Rico to:

1. Issue promptly independent audited financial statements (even if issued with qualified opinion); and
2. Provide monthly, publicly available, detailed reports of its revenues, expenses, cash-flows, debt, payroll, performance versus budget, level of governmental employment, and key labor and economic indicators.

This will provide essential information for the Authority to commence its work. One cannot fix, what one cannot measure or monitor.

I thank you for the privilege and honor to address you today. I would gladly answer any questions related to my testimony and offer my pro-bono collaboration for advancing the work of this committee and of this U.S. Congress in delivering practical and urgent relief measures to Puerto Rico.

Attachments (Reference Materials)

1. Puerto Rico Fiscal Restructuring and Stability Board Comprehensive Final Report to the Puerto Rico Legislature including Annexes, dated March 30, 2011 (in Spanish)

   [Due to size limitations (114 pages), this document is not included in this printed version. It is being retained in the Committee's official files.]

2. Puerto Rico Reconstruction Plan, dated March 5, 2009, as presented to the Puerto Rico Legislature (in English)

   [Due to size limitations (60 pages), this document is not included in this printed version. It is being retained in the Committee's official files.]

3. Puerto Rico Government Progress Report Presentation to the Obama Administration, dated November 23, 2010 (in English)

   [Due to size limitations (30 pages), this document is not included in this printed version. It is being retained in the Committee's official files.]

4. White Paper: "A Proposal to Jumpstart Economic Activity in Puerto Rico with a Minimal to Revenue Neutral Impact to U.S. Taxpayers" by Carlos Garcia, dated January 31, 2016 [See below]

*****

ATTACHMENT

"A Proposal to Jumpstart Economic Activity in Puerto Rico With a Minimal to Revenue Neutral Impact to U.S. Taxpayers"

By Carlos Garcia

January 31, 2016

WHITE PAPER

Proposal

U.S. taxpayers would be permitted to repatriate funds regarded as permanently invested outside the United States for financial accounting purposes up to $40 billion in the aggregate under the conditions that:

1. the repatriated funds would be subject to rules generally consistent with the rules of former section 965, which provided an elective, temporary 85-percent dividends-received deduction for certain dividends received by a domestic corporation from foreign controlled corporations, subject to various conditions and limitations; and

2. at least one half of the amount of such funds that are repatriated by any tax-payer are invested in assets used (or to be used within 5 years) in the active conduct of a trade or business carried on by the taxpayer (or an affiliate) in Puerto Rico or invested in activities or financial instruments that create jobs and promote economic activity in Puerto Rico, with priority given to the following:

   a. Developing energy and infrastructure projects;
   b. Facilitating the creation and expansion of small and medium-size businesses as well as the export of products and services;
   c. Furthering education at all levels;
   d. Conducting scientific and medical research;
   e. Creating a STEM innovation district;
   f. Creating a Latin American medical-tourism and veterinary hub;
   g. Reinvigorating local rum production and other agricultural products; and
   h. Promoting regional initiatives designed to make Puerto Rico a low-cost tourism alternative by among other means, re-developing the former Roosevelt Roads naval base and the Ramey air base, cleaning the Island of Vieques, etc.

Other Conditions and Considerations

As stated above, the repatriated funds would be subject to rules generally consistent with former Internal Revenue Code section 965, enacted in 2004 as part of the American Jobs Creation Act to provide a temporary tax holiday for repatriated corporate earnings. The rules, among other things, would provide an elective, temporary 85-percent dividends-received deduction for certain dividends received by a domestic corporation from foreign controlled corporations, subject to various conditions and limitations.

Because the aggregate amount of funds that could be repatriated is limited, a taxpayer would file an application with the U.S. Treasury Department, Office of the Fiscal Assistant Secretary, requesting permission to repatriate a specified amount of funds. The maximum amount that could be repatriated by a taxpayer (including all members of its affiliated group) would be $2 billion. Applications could be filed in the 120-day period following the date of enactment of the statute. If applications were filed for repatriations in excess of $40 billion, the Office of the Fiscal Assistant Secretary would have the authority to allocate the repatriations based upon criteria it would develop, including the number of jobs to be created in Puerto Rico and the purchases of goods and services in connection with the investment in the active conduct of a trade or business in Puerto Rico. If applications of less than $40 billion were filed, the Office of the Fiscal Assistant Secretary could extend the 120-day period for applications.

Revenue Estimate

I anticipate that the proposal will have only a minimal to revenue neutral effect on Federal income tax revenues, as per the analysis provided below and summarize on the attached table.

As background information, the Chief of Staff of the Joint Committee on Taxation in a letter to Senator Orrin Hatch dated June 6, 2014 estimated that if section 965 were re-enacted, based on the $1.5 trillion estimated amount of "offshore cash," tax revenues would be reduced by $95.8 billion for the period 2014 through 2024. The estimate was based on an analysis of the impact of the 2004 enactment of section 965.

The Joint Committee on Taxation noted four major factors at play in this estimate of revenue impact. The first was the loss in revenue associated with dividends that taxpayers would be predicted to repatriate even in the absence of enactment of the proposal. The second factor dealt with the U.S. tax effects associated with taxpayers changing their dividend repatriation amounts and/or timing in response to the proposal. There would be increases or decreases in revenues during the budget period based on whether repatriations were accelerated into the budget period. The third factor reflected the moral hazard problem if taxpayers anticipate that similar legislation may be enacted in the future that would enable them to repatriate dividends at a lower tax cost. The fourth factor was the predicted distribution of the repatriated funds to shareholders in the form of dividends or share repurchases, and the subsequent changes in individual income tax liability.

I would like to address the factors set out by the Joint Committee on Taxation in the context of this proposal. Under this proposal, the assumed repatriated amount would be $40 billion, which is 2.7% of the $1.5 trillion estimated "off-shore cash" in the Joint Committee study. A repatriation of $40 billion would result in an increase in tax receipts of $2.1 billion ($40 billion less 85% dividend received deduction on $40 billion times 35% tax rate) or 5.25% of $40 billion.

Of that repatriated amount, half ($20 billion) would have to be invested in Puerto Rico. This $20 billion results in tax receipts of $1.05 billion. Addressing the first and second factors in the Joint Committee study, it seems quite likely that that $20 billion required to be invested in Puerto Rico would not otherwise have been repatriated. Thus, without this repatriation plan, those tax receipts of $1.05 billion probably would never have been realized.

With respect to the $20 billion of the $40 billion that is not required to be invested in Puerto Rico, it may be reasonable to assume that 30% of the $20 billion ($6 billion) would have otherwise been repatriated. The maximum revenue loss with respect to such funds would be $1.785 billion ($6 billion times 35% tax rate less $6 billion times the 5.25% tax paid or $2.1 billion less $315 million). The increase in federal revenues on the remaining $14 billion that would not otherwise have been repatriated would be $735 million.

In these circumstances, the net revenue estimate for the proposal would be zero—$1.785 billion (maximum revenue loss on funds that would have been repatriated anyhow) less the sum of $1.05 billion and $735 million (revenue on funds that otherwise would not have been repatriated).

With respect to the third factor—moral hazard concern, because the proposal is targeted for very specific investments, it seems unlikely that there would be any moral hazard.

This revenue estimate does not consider fourth factor—the shareholder level effects of repatriation. It seems likely, however, that there would be additional collections of individual taxes from shareholders from the repatriation of funds, thereby further reducing the tax revenue estimate of the proposal.

In fact, given the design of the proposal, the likelihood of providing benefits to otherwise already planned repatriations is modest. As a consequence, there may be minimal revenue losses and perhaps even revenue gains from implementation of the proposal.

Economic Impact in Puerto Rico

Puerto Rico has suffered an economic depression now for over a decade. This proposal would be major step in reversing this decline. Puerto Rico's economy currently lacks funds for investment conducive to the generation of new economic activity and jobs. Upon successful implementation of this proposal, the investment of up to $20 billion through repatriation would represent in a period of 5 years a much needed injection of approximately 20% of Puerto Rico's gross domestic product (GDP) or an average of 4% of GDP per year. A more detailed analysis as to the economic impact and number of potential new jobs to be generated from this proposal could be provided upon request.

ILLUSTRATIVE TABLE - REVENUE ESTIMATES / IMPACT OF PROPOSAL ON FEDERAL TAX REVENUE

Assuming no change in law:

	Amount Repatriated (in billions)	Dividends Received Deduction %	Total Dividends Received Deduction	Tax Rate	Revenue
Amounts Repatriated Without Regard to Proposal	$6.00	0%	$0.00	35%	$2.10
				Total Revenue	$2.10 a

Assuming proposal is passed:

	Amount Repatriated (in billions)	Dividends Received Deduction %	Total Dividends Received Deduction	Tax Rate	Revenue
Amounts Repatriated Without Regard to Proposal	$6.00	85%	($5.10)	35%	$0.32
Investment in Puerto Rico Business	$20.00	85%	($17.00)	35%	$1.05
Other Amount Repatriated Not Invested in Puerto Rico	$14.00	85%	($11.90)	35%	$0.74
				Total Revenue	$2.10 b
				Total Lost Revenue	$0.00 a-b

Mr. YOUNG. Thank you, Mr. Garcia.

We now have Professor Simon Johnson.

STATEMENT OF SIMON JOHNSON, PROFESSOR OF GLOBAL ECONOMICS AND MANAGEMENT, MIT SLOANE SCHOOL OF MANAGEMENT, CAMBRIDGE, MASSACHUSETTS

Mr. JOHNSON. Thank you, Mr. Chairman. I am a professor at MIT's Sloane School of Management. I have worked on economic crises around the world for 30 years. In 2007 and 2008, I was the chief economist of the International Monetary Fund.

I would like to make three points. First of all, Mr. Chairman, I think you put your finger on the key issue already, which is if Puerto Rico were a state or had been allowed to become a state, we would not be here today. The safety mechanisms, the automatic stabilizers that states have in the United States, while not perfect, are not available to Puerto Rico. As a result, triggered in part by the economic crisis and other circumstances you have identified, when Puerto Rico started downhill, there was not enough force to pull it back up. Now we face what is, I'm afraid, an extremely serious debt crisis.

And I would emphasize, Mr. Chairman, one very important compounding factor, which I believe has never been seen to this extent in any other crisis around the world, and that is migration. There are 3½ million U.S. citizens. They will leave, and the people who leave are the people who pay taxes.

If the solution—and I don't believe it is what we are discussing today—but if the solution is austerity, wage cuts, benefits cut, they will leave. They will come to the United States, and they will take advantage, for example, of the earned income tax credit, which is a very good anti-poverty and pro-employment participation scheme that is available to everyone who lives in the 50 states, but not to people in Puerto Rico.

So in that context, I would emphasize—and I think I am agreeing with the two previous witnesses—these points. First of all, yes, a growth authority is a good idea under these circumstances. And, yes, audited financials and an understanding of exactly the situation today and realistic projections, of course that is absolutely a requirement. That is what every country in crisis needs.

But you have very little time. This is a serious crisis that has been growing for a long period, as you identified, Mr. Chairman. And I think Speaker Ryan is exactly right to emphasize that we need a plan, you need to act on legislation by the end of March. If you wait, the crisis will become considerably worse, more people will leave, the tax base will further disintegrate, and the creditors will get even less. Everyone loses in that situation.

The second point I would make is that I agree completely with Resident Commissioner Pierluisi on the issue of local democracy. Again, experience around the world is that when measures are taken under such difficult circumstances, if people feel that they are imposed from the outside, if local democracy is extinguished or felt to be extinguished, you do not have good outcomes. You have to have buy-in, and I think this is what Mr. Garcia was saying.

As a former constituent of Mr. Williams, I would say there was buy-in, and I would say he did a great job with the support of the local population. That is what you need to aim for in Puerto Rico. It is not easy, but I think there is a way forward as the Resident Commissioner has identified.

The third point, the most sensitive and perhaps the most emotional today, is the debt and the extent to which restructuring is needed and what kind of debt needs to be restructured. I think it is uncontroversial, but we will see, that the U.S. Government and Congress sits relative to Puerto Rico very much as a state sits relative to a city in other parts of the United States, in the 50 states.

And, you have the ability, the responsibility, and absolutely the legal authority to create a board or a growth authority that has the ability to restructure the debt and to potentially restructure all of the debt that has been issued by Puerto Rico. Obviously, not all creditors are the same, not all creditors have the same seniority, there are different terms, and different contracts. I really hope that a voluntary debt exchange can be agreed to.

But again, the experience around the world is that when you have a complex set of claims, as in Puerto Rico, and different kinds of creditors, they almost always have overly optimistic expectations about how much they can get if they wait and if they delay and if they don't agree to a voluntary exchange.

So, I think that you really must create the context of an authority that has this investigative ability, has the oversight ability, and does not extinguish democracy. That authority working, hopefully, with the established court system, which I think is very strong on many of these issues, must have the ability to restructure potentially all of the debt that has been issued by Puerto Rico. Thank you very much.

[The prepared statement of Mr. Johnson follows:]

PREPARED STATEMENT OF SIMON JOHNSON, RONALD KURTZ PROFESSOR OF ENTREPRENEURSHIP, MIT SLOAN SCHOOL OF MANAGEMENT; SENIOR FELLOW, PETERSON INSTITUTE FOR INTERNATIONAL ECONOMICS; AND CO-FOUNDER OF HTTP://BASELINESCENARIO.COM [1]

A. Main Points

1. Puerto Rico faces a serious and immediate debt crisis—scheduled payments have been missed, the government is forced to resort to emergency liquidity measures, and arrears to suppliers are building up.

2. Given recent economic outcomes and likely immediate prospects, it is clear that the government and its various agencies borrowed too much. At the same time, creditors must have been aware of the risks—Puerto Rico's economy has struggled over more than a decade and bond yields have long reflected the elevated risk of default.

3. The question now is how to put Puerto Rico back on the path to prosperity. A return to broad-based growth will permit rising living standards at the same time as ensuring the best possible outcomes for existing bondholders.

4. Puerto Rico needs a new set of economic policies—oriented toward boosting growth through reducing the cost of doing business and investing in productive opportunities.

5. One reaction is to demand further austerity, for example in the form of wage reductions and healthcare cuts. But residents of Puerto Rico are also U.S. citizens and they vote with their feet—the population has fallen from 3.9 million to 3.5 million in recent years as talented and energetic people have moved to Florida, Texas, and other parts of the mainland.

6. The situation is complicated by the fact that much of Puerto Rico's $70 billion debt was issued by government corporations.[2] Federal law allows such municipal debt to be restructured under Chapter 9 of the bankruptcy code in all 50 states but not in Puerto Rico, which is the largest U.S. terri-

---

[1] Also a member of the Federal Deposit Insurance Corporation's Systemic Resolution Advisory Committee, the Office of Financial Research's Financial Research Advisory Committee, and the independent Systemic Risk Council (created by Sheila Bair). All the views expressed here are mine alone. Underlined text indicates links to supplementary material; to see this, please access an electronic version of this document, e.g., at http://BaselineScenario.com. For important disclosures, see http://baselinescenario.com/about/.

[2] There are various estimates of the precise debt outstanding for which the government of Puerto Rico is responsible; $70 billion is a reasonable baseline number to use for gross public debt.

tory. A protracted series of confusing legal battles and selective defaults looms. The cost of essential infrastructure services—electricity, water, sewer, transportation—will go up while quality declines.

7. The more that creditors demand lower living standards and higher taxes, the more the tax base (i.e., people) will simply leave the island—and bondholders will only experience greater loss.

8. Disorganized public corporation default will also make it hard for any part of the private credit system to function. As private credit becomes harder to obtain, the real economy will decline further.

9. Leading voices—including at the Hoover Institution (http://www.hoover.org/research/lets-end-too-big-fail)—have long argued in favor of using established court-run process when large financial firms fail.[3] The same logic applies here: a judge can rely on precedent and ensure fairness across creditor classes, based on seniority and the precise terms under which loans were obtained.

10. A judge—for example, responsible for administering a broad restructuring authority—can remove any doubt that actual insolvency in fact exists, while also ensuring that credit remains available during a restructuring. A well-designed restructuring authority can also forestall disruptive litigation and prevent holdouts by a few creditors.

11. For a sustained economic recovery, Puerto Rico needs private sector investment, and this requires three steps.

    a. First, bureaucratic hurdles to job creation should be eliminated, including by using state-of-the-art technology to make government more transparent.

    b. Second, the cost of essential inputs for industry needs to fall. Electricity on Puerto Rico is significantly more expensive than in Florida, in part because of underinvestment. More broadly, there are pressing needs for public investment to improve infrastructure and this includes great opportunities for private sector participation—but none of this will happen until the debt overhang is removed.

    c. Third, Puerto Rico needs better fiscal management. The island's idiosyncratic tax and expenditure system—and the lack of effective local fiscal control—has become part of the longer-term problem. Puerto Rico should, over time, become more like one of the 50 states in its fiscal relationship with the Federal Government. If Congress is willing to commit to that path, a reasonable quid pro quo would be strong fiscal rules—and a powerful monitoring body.

12. With congressional support and pro-growth policies, Puerto Rico can attract talented Americans (and legal immigrants) to move to the island, to start companies, and to work hard. Higher education in Puerto Rico remains strong—but over 80,000 people leave to live and work elsewhere every year (while only 20,000 move in).

13. In part this is because the healthcare system in Puerto Rico is badly frayed. The Federal Government provides significantly more support to every state healthcare system through Medicaid and Medicare, despite the fact that Puerto Ricans pay the same Federal payroll taxes that fund much of the Medicare program.

14. And hard-working low income Puerto Ricans are eligible for more robust support, including through the earned income tax credit (EITC)—a program supported by leading conservatives, such as Speaker of the House of Representatives Paul Ryan—but only if they move to one of the 50 states.

15. Puerto Rico does not need a bailout. It needs to reduce the cost of doing business, encourage investment, and attract people to work (and pay tax). It also needs to move away from an unsustainable fiscal deal vis-à-vis the Federal Government—and toward the same kind of arrangement that is available to all 50 states.

---

[3] There is a debate about whether bankruptcy can be used to deal with the largest financial firms, because of potential systemic risk spillover effects—i.e., the failure of one firm causes other firms to fail. These concerns do not seem to apply in the case of Puerto Rico's debt.

B. Lessons from International Experience

Puerto Rico's current situation is unusual for the United States, but there are definite recent parallels with the experience of countries around the world.

Governments borrow when times are good—or when investors are willing to bet on an improvement in economic conditions. Some of this borrowing may be directly onto the government's balance sheet, but it is also quite common to take on debt through various quasi-government agencies that have an explicit or implicit guarantee.

During a boom, investors are typically willing to ignore or play down the potential risks—and there is not enough thinking about what exactly will happen in a downside scenario.

As credit conditions tighten and expectations become more pessimistic, bond yields go up—reflecting the additional risks. As this happens, it is quite common for a different kind of investor to become involved, e.g., hedge funds. The risks of default are clearly higher but some investors still feel that the additional return justifies buying the debt.

At this stage, there is usually an active secondary market for debt—as investors who like risk buy up debt at a deep discount. Some investors may also take the view that they are acquiring more senior claims—or claims that will have advantageous treatment in the event of a restructuring.

When a country loses access to debt markets and is generally regarded as having unsustainable fiscal policies, some form of crisis ensues.

The main issue then becomes: How much will the existing debt be restructured? At the country-level there is a longstanding problem because there is no agreed mechanism (or court-run process) to determine a fair amount of debt reduction. As a result, there is reliance in the first instance on voluntary debt swaps (e.g., reducing the present value of payments but not always lowering principal). If this approach does not work, the International Monetary Fund often becomes involved—and the extent and nature of IMF support becomes part of the conversation with creditors.

IMF support comes with strings attached, including detailed monitoring of fiscal flows (and related monetary developments). However, IMF programs only work when there is substantial local buy-in. Imposing austerity from outside is never a good idea.

The viability of any IMF program (and related international assistance) always depends on getting debt payments down to a sustainable level. In this context, it is best if the payments can be made contingent on outcomes, i.e., if the economy recovers, then bondholders receive more.

A sovereign debt restructuring mechanism (SDRM) has been proposed in the past—and was given serious consideration by the George W. Bush administration. Unfortunately, we do not currently have an SDRM at the international level—and this makes debt restructuring more time consuming and harder to implement. In particular, some investors decide to hold out for full repayment and this can greatly complicate a return to capital markets for the government.

Compared with international experiences, Puerto Rico has the potential advantage that a restructuring mechanism could be put in place. Municipal bankruptcy (within the United States) is one obvious precedent, but a broader process—to include all debt—may also be considered.

In any such process, not all creditors will be treated alike—depending on the precise nature of the commitment to pay them (seniority of claim, broadly defined). The point is to have a fair, transparent, and politically legitimate process to decide on these payments. Running such a process through a judge (and the court system) has a great deal of appeal in the United States.

All such debt restructurings are contentious and no one ends up completely happy. But creditors were taking on well-documented risks when they lent to Puerto Rico. And the Federal Government has long made it clear that it does not stand behind the obligations of states or state-backed municipal lenders.

The reaction of debt markets to developments in Puerto Rico so far has been muted—and this is further confirmation that investors understand the risks with this kind of lending are quite differentiated across borrowers.

The biggest danger for Puerto Rico is that there will be no comprehensive debt restructuring. Without further congressional action, the terms on some loans will be changed, but only partially and likely not enough to return the territory to fiscal sustainability.

One potential historical parallel is Latin America during the 1980s. Following a debt crisis that began in 1982, there was a long period of stagnation—until the U.S. Treasury helped to facilitate a restructuring at the end of the decade.

Puerto Rico could easily experience a lost decade of growth. And outcomes (in terms of economic aggregates in Puerto Rico) could even be dramatic because residents can move to the 50 states. In modern times we have never experienced this particular dimension of a debt crisis—the relatively easy exit of a population.[4]

International experience teaches us that economic recoveries are possible, even from apparently dire circumstances. Puerto Rico does not have its own currency, so recovery through devaluation is not an option. And reducing wages in Puerto Rico would induce more people to leave—this should be regarded as an important constraint on policy.

But international experience also suggests there is a sensible way forward if Congress and the government of Puerto Rico are willing to support: significant debt restructuring in a court-run process; improvement in fiscal management, including with external oversight; a reduction in the cost of doing business; and an investment-led recovery.

———

Mr. YOUNG. I hope we have the intelligence to call upon these witnesses to help us write a piece of legislation because I can guarantee if we write it by ourselves, we will screw it up.

So, Mr. Eric LeCompte.

STATEMENT OF ERIC LeCOMPTE, EXECUTIVE DIRECTOR, JUBILEE USA NETWORK, WASHINGTON, DC

Mr. LeCOMPTE. I truly appreciate your opening comments in terms of framing the crisis and the situation that we are dealing with. I also want to thank the previous panelists and also certainly identify my remarks with Professor Simon Johnson's, who I think gave a very good assessment of the needs and the situation.

Mr. YOUNG. Eric, excuse me, you with the gray hair, would you quit bobbing around? It bothers me when people are testifying. When someone is testifying, I don't like distractions.

Go ahead, Eric.

Mr. LeCOMPTE. I am the Executive Director of Jubilee USA. We represent national religious bodies, congregations, and institutions. Our founders and member groups in the United States range from the U.S. Conference of Catholic Bishops, to American Jewish World Service, to most of the national protestant denominations. We represent 550 faith communities across our great country, and we focus on how the most vulnerable are impacted by global issues such as trade, debt, corruption, and taxes.

We have worked with Congress and successive administrations on global debt issues for almost 20 years. Because of the agreements we have achieved together, our financial system is more responsible and transparent, and developing countries have seen over $130 billion in debt relief to build schools and medical centers around the world.

It is thanks to President George W. Bush that in 2005 the cornerstone of U.S. bipartisan policy on debt restructuring and financial accountability was laid, the Multi-Lateral Debt Relief Initiative. Not only did this legislation enable innovative financing to countries who needed to deal with poor populations, it also set standards around government accountability and public budget transparency.

---

[4] Some euro area countries now experience substantial out-migration, including for young and educated people. But it is harder to move within the euro area—for cultural and linguistic reasons—than it is to move from Puerto Rico to Florida, Texas, or other states.

In Puerto Rico, in particular, we partnered with religious leaders representing more than 95 percent of the island's population. The leaders include the Catholic Archbishop of San Juan and the head of Puerto Rico's Bible Society. Along with my testimony, I submit an August statement signed by all of Puerto Rico's major religious leaders asking Congress to take action regarding the crisis in Puerto Rico. I also submit a letter from Archbishop Wenski on behalf of the U.S. Conference of Catholic Bishops urging Congress to pass bankruptcy protection for the indebted territory.

From a religious perspective, we recognize, as you laid out, Chairman Young, that this is not simply a debt crisis; this is a humanitarian crisis. Consider that nearly 50 percent of Puerto Rico's people live in poverty, 50 percent of Puerto Rico's children live in homes that receive some form of welfare benefits, and 80 percent of Puerto Rico's children live in high poverty areas. Because pension accounts have been used to pay the debt, government pensions may not have enough funds to meet their obligations by 2020; the current unemployment rate of Puerto Rico is over 12 percent; and over the past decade, 10 percent of the population has left for the U.S. mainland in search of work.

Like our religious partners on the island, we pray for two things: first, long-term solutions to Puerto Rico's economic troubles that address the underlying problems that led to this mess in the first place; and second, immediate measures to help Puerto Rico's people who are suffering right now.

This committee has a very important role to play in both the short term and long term. In the short term, the reality is that Puerto Rico cannot cut its way out of this crisis. It cannot tax its way out of this crisis. There is no path to economic growth in Puerto Rico that does not start with debt restructuring.

Self-imposed austerity in Puerto Rico is already proving harmful and counterproductive. Funding for law enforcement has dropped 3 years in a row; special education teachers are no longer being paid, directly harming some of the most vulnerable kids on the island; 200 schools have closed; Puerto Rico cut its health spending by $42 million this year, and this takes place as the Zika virus now spreads in Puerto Rico.

These types of measures push more people on the island to leave for the U.S. mainland, which further erodes Puerto Rico's tax base. It is a cycle that is only getting worse.

The good news is that we can solve this crisis in ways that promote economic growth and reduce child poverty. A step in this direction is enacting bankruptcy protection for Puerto Rico, the same type of protection U.S. municipalities have access to. We applaud the efforts of Representatives Duffy and Pierluisi for introducing bankruptcy legislation. We are very grateful to Speaker Ryan for setting a timeline for action.

Our opposition to austerity should not be confused with opposition to reform. At the root of today's hearing lies the question: How do we prevent future debt crises in Puerto Rico, and how do we ensure greater accountability from Puerto Rico's government?

Part of the answer to this question is that through an orderly debt restructuring process we bring the debt back to sustainable, payable levels. However, this committee is concerned also with how there needs to be more accountability from Puerto Rico's government itself.

From the beginning of this crisis, Jubilee USA and its religious partners in Puerto Rico called for increased budget transparency and accountability in the island's government. We want more citizens' participation in economic decisionmaking, policies that we have pursued successfully on other heavily-indebted Caribbean islands and countries around the world.

To this end, we are pleased that the Puerto Rico Audit Commission has begun its work. We support Congress' action to make available Treasury's Office of Technical Assistance. This particular action that you all enacted with the omnibus can help Puerto Rico keep its debt stock in order, become more accountable to its citizens, and raise revenues. This action can show powerful results.

I think, in closing, in terms of the question of the financial control board that this committee is looking at today, we have seen this type of fiscal authority utilized during other economic crises in the United States. In terms of Puerto Rico, the White House has acknowledged the need for some authority, and Representative Duffy's legislation details how one would be constructed.

As Congress looks to pass bankruptcy and greater accountability provisions, any control board must look at how Puerto Rico is represented in the process. If Congress passes bankruptcy protection with a control board, Congress should ensure that such a control board is co-chaired by appointments from the Federal Government and the government of Puerto Rico. Local democracy must be respected.

In the long term, we believe the island needs reforms that will ensure that Puerto Rico's economy serves its people, debt restructuring to allow for economic growth, and accountability measures to stave corruption. Currently, 3.5 million Americans face a humanitarian crisis. We look forward to working with the committee to find a solution to end the crisis, promote economic growth, and ensure greater transparency.

Thank you, Mr. Chairman.

[The prepared statement of Mr. LeCompte follows:]

PREPARED STATEMENT OF ERIC LECOMPTE, EXECUTIVE DIRECTOR, JUBILEE USA NETWORK

Thank you Chairman Young, Ranking Member Grijalva and members of the committee.

I am the Executive Director of Jubilee USA—and we represent national U.S. religious bodies, congregations and institutions. Our founders and member groups range from the U.S. Conference of Catholic Bishops to American Jewish World Service to most of the national Protestant denominations. We represent 550 faith communities across our great country. We focus on how the most vulnerable are impacted by global issues such as trade, debt, corruption and taxes.

We've worked with Congress and successive administrations on global debt issues for almost 20 years. Because of the agreements we've achieved together, our financial system is more responsible and transparent and developing countries have seen over $130 billion in debt relief to build schools and medical centers. It is thanks to President George W. Bush that in 2005 the cornerstone of U.S. policy on debt restructuring and financial accountability was laid, the Multi-Lateral Debt Relief Initiative (MDRI). Not only did this legislation enable innovative financing to countries who need it most for poor populations, it also set standards around government accountability and public budget transparency.

In Puerto Rico we partner with religious leaders representing more than 95 percent of the island's people. These leaders include the Catholic Archbishop of

San Juan and the head of Puerto Rico's Bible Society. Along with my testimony, I submit an August statement signed by all of Puerto Rico's major religious leaders asking Congress to take action regarding the crisis in Puerto Rico. I also submit a letter from Archbishop Wenski on behalf of the U.S. Conference of Catholic Bishops urging Congress to pass bankruptcy protection for the indebted territory.

From a religious perspective, we recognize that this is not simply a debt crisis— this is a humanitarian crisis. Consider:

- Nearly 50 percent of Puerto Rico's people live in poverty;
- 50 percent of Puerto Rico's children live in homes that receive some form of welfare benefits;
- 80 percent of Puerto Rico's children live in high-poverty areas;
- Because pension accounts have been used to pay the debt, government pensions may not have enough funds to meet their obligations by 2020;
- The current unemployment rate in Puerto Rico is over 12 percent;
- Over the past decade, 10 percent of the population has left for the U.S. mainland in search of work.

Like our religious partners on the island, we pray for two things:

First: long-term solutions to Puerto Rico's economic troubles that address the underlying problems that led the island into this mess in the first place.

Second: immediate measures to help Puerto Rico's people who are suffering right now.

This committee has an important role to play in both the short-term and the long-term.

In the short-term, the reality is, Puerto Rico can't cut its way out of this crisis. It can't tax its way out of this crisis. There is no path to economic growth for Puerto Rico that doesn't include debt restructuring.

Self-imposed austerity in Puerto Rico is already proving harmful and counter-productive:

- Funding for law enforcement has dropped 3 years in a row;
- Special education teachers are no longer being paid, directly harming some of the most vulnerable kids on the island;
- 200 schools have closed;
- Puerto Rico cut its health spending by $42 million this year. This takes place as the Zika virus now spreads in Puerto Rico.

These types of measures push more people on the island to leave for the U.S. Mainland, which further erodes Puerto Rico's tax base. It's a cycle that's only getting worse.

The good news is that we can solve this crisis in ways that promote economic growth and reduce child poverty. A step in this direction is enacting bankruptcy protection for Puerto Rico—the same type of protection U.S. municipalities have access to. We applaud the efforts of Representatives Duffy and Pierluisi for introducing bankruptcy legislation. We are grateful to Speaker Ryan for setting a timeline for action.

Our opposition to austerity should not be confused with opposition to reform.

At the root of today's hearing lie the questions, "How do we prevent future debt crises in Puerto Rico and how do we ensure greater accountability from Puerto Rico's government?"

Part of the answer to this question is that through an orderly debt restructuring process we bring the debt back to sustainable, payable levels. However, this committee is concerned also with how there is more accountability from Puerto Rico's government.

From the beginning of this crisis, Jubilee USA and its religious partners in Puerto Rico called for increased budget transparency and accountability in the island's government. We want more citizen participation in economic decisionmaking, policies that we've pursued successfully on other heavily indebted Caribbean islands and countries around the world. To this end, we are pleased with that Puerto Rico's audit commission has begun its work.

We also believe that Congress should make immediately available Treasury's Office of Technical Assistance (OTA) to the government of Puerto Rico. Because of Puerto Rico's status, it can't access this vital expertise from Treasury that helps countries all over the world raise revenues, keep their debt stock in order and become more accountable to their citizens. This is an easy action Congress can take that would show powerful results.

In terms of the financial control board that this committee is looking at today. We've seen this type of fiscal authority utilized during other economic crises in the United States. In terms of Puerto Rico, the White House has acknowledged the need for some authority and Representative Duffy's legislation details how one would be constructed. As Congress looks to pass bankruptcy and greater accountability provisions, any control board must look at how Puerto Rico is represented in the process. If Congress passes bankruptcy protection with a control board, Congress should ensure that such a control board is co-chaired by appointments from the Federal Government and the government of Puerto Rico.

In the long-run, we believe the island needs reforms that ensure Puerto Rico's economy serves its people, debt restructuring that invests in economic growth and accountability measures that stave corruption—3.5 million Americans face a humanitarian crisis. We look forward to working with the committee to find a solution to end the crisis, promote economic growth and ensure greater transparency.

Thank you.

Attachments:

Letter from U.S. Conference of Catholic Bishops to Congress in support of legislation granting Puerto Rico access to Chapter 9 bankruptcy protection

Statement from Puerto Rico religious leaders calling for solutions to the island's debt crisis

*****

ATTACHMENTS

COMMITTEE ON DOMESTIC JUSTICE AND HUMAN DEVELOPMENT,
WASHINGTON, DC,

DECEMBER 1, 2015.

United States Senate,
Washington, DC 20510.

DEAR SENATOR:

The people of Puerto Rico are suffering from painful poverty and hunger, persistent joblessness, and other social problems, as a result of the financial crisis gripping the Commonwealth's economy. They bear little responsibility for the situation yet suffer most of the consequences. Congress can and should remedy this situation by advancing the Puerto Rico Chapter 9 Uniformity Act.

The *Compendium of the Social Doctrine of the Church* teaches:

> The right to development must be taken into account when considering questions related to the debt crisis of many poor countries . . . Complex causes of various types lie at the origin of the debt crisis, [but] . . . [t]he greatest sufferings, which can be traced back both to structural questions as well as personal behaviour, strike the people of poor and indebted countries who are not responsible for this situation. The international community cannot ignore this fact . . . (No. 450)

Earlier this year, Pope Francis affirmed this to the General Assembly of the United Nations, decrying lending systems that "subject people to mechanisms which generate greater poverty, exclusion and dependence." Financial instruments should encourage development, not deprivation. We all have a shared responsibility to protect our poor and vulnerable brothers and sisters around the world.

The government of Puerto Rico's political status has made it difficult to fulfill adequately its obligation to ensure human needs are met and advance the common good. Because it is not a sovereign nation, it cannot access financial assistance from the International Monetary Fund; because it is not a state, federal law exempts it from crucial protections in the bankruptcy code. With virtually no other option at its disposal currently, Puerto Rico remains at the mercy of creditors with seemingly little concern for the pain and suffering caused to the people and families of Puerto Rico.

The Bankruptcy Code explicitly and inexplicably excludes Puerto Rico from the definition of 'state' for the purpose of seeking protection under Chapter 9. The Puerto Rico Chapter 9 Uniformity Act would allow the Puerto Rican people, through their government, to take greater control of their development and destiny. I encourage you to support this legislation.

Sincerely,

MOST REVEREND THOMAS G. WENSKI,
Chairman.

***

A CALL FROM THE ECUMENICAL AND INTER-RELIGIOUS COALITION AND OTHER RELIGIOUS LEADERS FOR A JUBILEE FOR PUERTO RICO: THE FISCAL CRISIS

AUGUST 31, 2015

Brothers and Sisters,

Puerto Rico is embroiled in a debt crisis. This crisis further threatens nearly half of our people living in poverty. As leaders of the faith community, we are concerned about the debt, with the consequences defaulting on it and above all with the proposals that would reduce wages, layoffs of workers, reducing employee benefits, and a reduction in health services. As a society, we cannot allow more austerity measures that adversely affect the poor and needy in Puerto Rico. Those who lend money at high interest rates knowing that it is a heavy burden to the fiscal health of the people have no moral strength to demand austerity measures affecting essential services, jobs and opportunities of an economic resurgence.

We know how complicated these issues and their causes are. Our country is $72 billion in debt and that represents $20,000 of debt for every man, woman and child of Puerto Rico. Not only has the debt already impacted our social services, too many of our people are fleeing to the United States in search of work. As we struggle, we are also concerned with predatory hedge funds which seek to benefit from our distress and push our economy to the brink of collapse.

Today, we look to the Bible for a solution. The solution first appears in Leviticus and becomes a central theme in the Gospels. The solution is Jubilee:

> ". . . and you shall consecrate the fiftieth year and proclaim liberty throughout the land to all its inhabitants. It shall be a jubilee for you, when each of you shall return to his property . . ." (Leviticus 25:10)

And then reiterated by Christ's first public act in Luke, where he said the prophesy of Isaiah to end inequality was fulfilled:

> "THE SPIRIT OF THE LORD IS UPON ME, BECAUSE HE ANOINTED ME TO PREACH THE GOSPEL TO THE POOR. HE HAS SENT ME TO PROCLAIM RELEASE TO THE CAPTIVES, AND RECOVERY OF SIGHT TO THE BLIND, TO SET FREE THOSE WHO ARE OPPRESSED, TO PROCLAIM THE FAVORABLE YEAR OF THE LORD." (Luke 4:18–19)

Today we too call for a JUBILEE. We call for freedom from debt, for relief for our people. As Isaiah and Jesus called, we call for a Jubilee for Puerto Rico's people. We are a part of a story bigger than just us.

In the 1990s, religious leaders called for a Jubilee or debt relief for developing countries. Those calls ensured that more than $115 billion in debt relief was won to create access to education and healthcare. Now as Puerto Rico faces a debt crisis, as the religious community, we raise our voices for Jubilee. Puerto Rico needs debt relief and a debt restructuring that invests in Puerto Rico's people.

As religious leaders we know how deeply this crisis impacts the poor and how deeply it impacts all of our people. We ask that the following principles guide how this financial crisis is resolved:

1. In any solution that is reached, there should be no more austerity policies affecting people and poor families and young people who are the most vulnerable.

2. Any solution must create an investment in the Puerto Rican people and seek to grow our economy.

3. We need enough debt relief to bring our total debt back to sustainable levels.

4. We encourage all solutions that enhance Puerto Rico's laws on budget transparency.

5. We seek greater participation in resolving this crisis and working with the government on solutions that protect Puerto Rico's people.

6. In addition to the participation of the religious sector, we call for a multi-sectorial participation in which our people are well represented. A representation that also includes the poorest because they are always the most affected.

We understand that some processes and options typically available to indebted governments are not available to ours. Because Puerto Rico is not a sovereign country, we can't receive low-interest loans or emergency financing from the International Monetary Fund. Because Puerto Rico is not a U.S. state or city, we can't access U.S. bankruptcy laws. In the absence of Congress extending bankruptcy protection to Puerto Rico, we must call for greater involvement from the Federal Reserve to act and to arbitrate our debt according to our six principles to protect the common good. The Federal Reserve has the power to act and should act. The Federal Reserve has the ability to restructure our debt in ways that limit austerity and ensure debt relief without harmful conditions.

As we call for a Jubilee for Puerto Rico's people, we call for a Jubilee for all people. We call for economies to serve people, not for people to serve economies.

Puerto Rico is not alone in its suffering from debt. Our brothers and sisters in the Caribbean are facing high debt burdens and poverty rates made worse by increasingly frequent storms. Farther south, Argentina continues its standoff with hedge funds that pushed it into default as part of a messy debt dispute. Nearly 50 of the world's poorest countries face worrying levels of debt distress. We've even seen debt and austerity push a third of Greece's population below the poverty line. We call for a global bankruptcy process that addresses debt crises in every corner of the world, whether they be in the Caribbean, Africa or Eastern Europe.

As people of faith we are called to be present always to the most vulnerable among us. As people of faith, we believe that we are closest to the Creator when we are sharing God's abundant creation among us. As people of faith we pray for an end of poverty and inequality. As people of faith, we call for relief and Jubilee for all people.

Mons. Roberto O. González Nieves,
Metropolitan Archbishop of San
   Juan de Puerto Rico

Rev. Heriberto Martínez Rivera,
General Secretary—Bible Society of
   Puerto Rico

Mons. Rubén González Medina CMF,
Bishop of Caguas

Rev. Juan A. Vera Mendez,
Emeritus Bishop, Methodist Church
   of Puerto Rico

Mons. Félix Lázaro Martínez, Sc. P.,
Bishop of Ponce

Rev. Rafael Moreno Rivas,
Bishop—Methodist Church in P.R.
   President of P.R. Council of
   Churches

Mons. Álvaro Corrada del Río, S.J.,
Bishop of Mayaguez

Rev. Felipe Lozada Montañez,
Bishop—Evangelic Lutheran Church
   in Puerto Rico

Mons. Eusebio Ramos Morales,
Bishop of Fajardo-Humacao

Rev. Miguel A. Morales Castro,
General Pastor—Christian Church
   (Disciples of Christ) in P.R.

Rev. Adalberto Rodríguez,
President—Pentecostal Fraternity of
   Puerto Rico

Rev. Edward Rivera Santiago,
General Pastor—United Evangelical
   Church of Puerto Rico

Rev. Roberto Dieppa Báez,
Executive Minister—Baptist
   Churches of Puerto Rico

Rev. Héctor Soto Vélez,
Executive Secretary—Council of
   Churches of Puerto Rico

Rev. Eunice Santana Melecio,
Director—Caribbean Inst. of
   Ecumenical Action and Formation

Rev. Ricardo Cortés Alemán,
Missions Director—Defenders of the
   Christian Faith of Puerto Rico

Rev. Ricardo López Ortiz Rev.,
Administrator Bishop—Church of
   God Mission Board of P.R. Church

Esteban González Dobles,
Former General Pastor—Christian
   (Disciples of Christ) in P.R.

———

Mr. YOUNG. Thank you, sir.

Mr. Mayer, you are last, but I am not going to say that you are best yet. We will see what happens.

STATEMENT OF THOMAS MOERS MAYER, PARTNER, KRAMER LEVIN NAFTALIS & FRANKEL, LLP, NEW YORK, NEW YORK

Mr. MAYER. Thank you, Chairman Young, Ranking Member Ruiz, and the members of the subcommittee for inviting me to testify today. My name is Thomas Moers Mayer, and I represent mutual funds managed by Franklin Advisers and Oppenheimer Funds that collectively own $10 billion of Puerto Rico debt securities. We think we are the largest creditors of the island.

We invest on behalf of hundreds of thousands of individual investors. Franklin and Oppenheimer collectively have over 600,000 shareholders in their municipal bond funds—and municipal bond investors, ladies and gentlemen, they are individuals. Most Puerto Rican debt is held by individuals, including as Representative Pierluisi acknowledged, Puerto Ricans themselves both on- and off-island, and these investors, they are mostly over 65, and they mostly have an income of less than $100,000 a year. They are not vulture funds. They are your friends and neighbors, and they are not the problem.

We believe that a substantial amount of the problem, perhaps all of the problem, is found in misgovernment and not in investment. The Commonwealth itself fails to collect $2.5 billion a year in taxes that its own consultants say it has the ability to collect. At the governmental corporation level, the electric company, PREPA, with which I am quite familiar, it sells power to government corporations that do not pay. It pays an annual salary to employees for as little as 9 months work, and it is run by 200 political appointees.

A bipartisan authority, a strong authority, can address these problems. We would urge that this authority be appointed by the President, confirmed by the Senate, and it must be acceptable to Puerto Rico. We believe the authority should have the power to address the problems that need to be addressed, most particularly the power of the purse. Access to Federal funds should be conditioned on the authority approval of Puerto Rico's budget. That is exactly the setup that applied in the DC Control Board.

With respect to government-operating corporations like the electric company, sewer company, and the highway company, these are the entities that Chapter 9 applies to. I will come back to that. The authority needs to have the power to fix the problems, the power to fire and hire and renegotiate contracts, restructure pensions, and restructure operations. And when it has done that, yes, then we think it should have the power to restructure its debt with a majority of the bondholders voting in favor, which is I think something the IMF has tried to install in the international arena.

The one power neither the authority nor Puerto Rico should have, in our view, is access to Chapter 9. Chapter 9 is a way to avoid reforms rather than implement them, and we think it causes far more problems than it solves.

First, it does not help. The crisis that everybody refers to is in the general government. Chapter 9 does not apply to the general government—and no one that I've heard in Congress, including Representative Pierluisi, has suggested that it should—because then it would be equivalent to applying Chapter 9 to a state, which Congress has never done.

So, with respect to the government corporations that Chapter 9 would apply to, let's enumerate the problems. First, it does not raise money. Every now and then I hear that corporations can go into bankruptcy and they can raise money. Well, I have been practicing bankruptcy law a long time, and lenders do not lend money in any bankrupt situation unless they have collateral. And with respect to the government corporations in Puerto Rico, there is no collateral. All the money has been pledged to the bondholders.

The only source of liquidity is a deal with the bondholders; and we have such a deal. We have a deal at the Puerto Rican Electric Power Authority. We negotiated it months ago. It is waiting for legislation in Puerto Rico to be effectuated. There was a liquidity problem at the Puerto Rican Electric Power Authority, and we fixed it. We loaned the money. We suggest that as a template for how to deal with Puerto Rico's other governmental corporations.

Chapter 9 does not implement reforms. I ask you to compare the experience of the District of Columbia with the city of Detroit. The District of Columbia, actually there was a consideration of giving DC Chapter 9. It is in their congressional reports, and it was debated. And Congress said no, Chapter 9 does not fix problems. So they established a control board, and the control board did what needed to be done. It cut the size of government. It eliminated the deficit, turned it to surplus, brought the bonds back to investment grade. The private sector flourished, and the results you have today, the District is an AA-rated entity.

Now let's take a look at Detroit, which some people like to mention as a success. Detroit went into Chapter 9, and it used Chapter 9 to crush its bondholders, to largely isolate the pensions from any change. It went into Chapter 9 with 28 city agencies, and it came out of Chapter 9 with 28 city agencies. And as a result today, despite what you may have heard, Detroit has no access to municipal finance. It can only borrow through the state of Michigan. Detroit's own paper trades at 23 cents on the dollar.

Like Detroit, Puerto Rico has a gross abundance of government agencies. It has 120 government agencies, which one of the witnesses testified he could not fix. If you give Chapter 9 to Puerto Rico, it will not reduce this problem. And unlike Detroit, Puerto Rico does not have Michigan. It has the Federal Government. If you give it Chapter 9, it is going to be back. My people have been investing in Puerto Rico for 30 years. We would like to invest for another 30 years. We are not short-term players. We look forward to working with this committee to craft a solution that works for everyone. Thank you.

[The prepared statement of Mr. Mayer follows:]

PREPARED STATEMENT OF THOMAS MOERS MAYER, PARTNER AND CO-CHAIR, CORPORATE RESTRUCTURING AND BANKRUPTCY GROUP, KRAMER LEVIN NAFTALIS & FRANKEL, LLP, NEW YORK, NY

Chairman Young, Ranking Member Ruiz, and members of the subcommittee—thank you for inviting me to testify on the Need for the Establishment of a Puerto Rico Financial Stability and Economic Growth Authority, which I will refer to as an "Authority."

My name is Thomas Moers Mayer.[1] I have spent the better part of a decade working on municipal insolvencies and observing how municipal insolvencies work in and out of bankruptcy, and I have spent the last year examining the Commonwealth's fiscal situation and economy in light of its claim that it cannot pay its bondholders.

I offer that experience and my views today on behalf of my clients, certain funds managed by Franklin Advisers ("Franklin") and by OppenheimerFunds, Inc. ("Oppenheimer") in connection with their investment in approximately $10 billion of bonds issued by the Commonwealth of Puerto Rico and most of its 16 governmental corporations.

WHO INVESTS IN PUERTO RICO?

Franklin and Oppenheimer have for many years been two of the largest investors in bonds issued by Puerto Rico and its governmental corporations; to the best of my knowledge, my clients collectively constitute the largest holders of Puerto Rico bonds.

Franklin and Oppenheimer are mutual funds who invest on behalf of hundreds of thousands of retail investors. Franklin alone has approximately 200,000 investors in the funds that own bonds issued by Puerto Rico and its government corporations; Oppenheimer has over 400,000 individual investors in its municipal bond funds, most of which hold Puerto Rico bonds.

These bondholders are individual savers who receive tax-exempt income derived from Puerto Rico municipal bond holdings. Most tax returns showing tax-exempt income are filed by taxpayers over 65[2] and most report incomes under $100,000.[3] The average investment in one of Oppenheimer's funds is $50,000.

These people live on Main Street, not Wall Street.[4] These investors are ordinary people who invest for retirement and for their children's education. They are taxpayers who want to buy tax-free bonds. Indeed, about 9.5 million U.S. taxpayers invest in municipal bonds to get tax-free income, either directly or through funds like Franklin's and Oppenheimer's.[5]

Puerto Rico is the only large issuer whose bonds are tax-free in every state of the union,[6] and it is likely that most municipal bondholders (or fund holders) hold, directly or indirectly, Puerto Rico bonds.

---

[1] I am a partner and co-chair of the Corporate Restructuring and Bankruptcy Group at Kramer Levin Naftalis & Frankel, LLP. *See* Exhibit A. I am also a member of the National Bankruptcy Conference (the "NBC"), which provided its own statement in support of a predecessor to H.R. 870. I was not a signatory to the NBC's statement and abstained from a vote on it. My testimony today is not on behalf of the NBC, which has not reviewed it.

[2] *Statistics of Income, 2013 Individual Income Tax Returns*, Publ. 1304, U.S. DEP'T OF THE TREASURY, INTERNAL REVENUE SERVICE, Table 1.5 at 81 (2013), https://www.irs.gov/pub/irs-soi/13inalcr.pdf (hereinafter "*IRS Publ. 1304*").

[3] *Id*. Table 1.4 at 43.

[4] The "household sector" held almost 42% of all municipal bonds as of September 30, 2015. *Federal Reserve Statistical Release Z.1, Financial Accounts of the United States, Flow of Funds, Balance Sheets, and Integrated Macroeconomic Accounts, Third Quarter 2015*, Bd. of Governors of the Fed. Reserve Sys. 101 (Dec. 10, 2015), http://www.federalreserve.gov/releases/z1/current/z1.pdf. Mutual funds together held an additional 19%. *Id*.

[5] In 2013, 5,987,263 tax returns reported tax exempt income, comprised of 3,556,447 tax returns from married couples filing jointly, or 7,112,894 individuals, and 2,430,817 other individual tax returns, for a total of 9,543,711 individuals. *IRS Publ. 1304*, supra note 2, Table 1.3 at 40.

[6] *See* 48 U.S.C. § 745.

These investors bought their bonds after Congress expressly excluded Puerto Rico from using Chapter 9. My own clients—on behalf of more than half a million investors—bought their bonds in reliance on Puerto Rico's exclusion from Chapter 9.

How Congress decides to address Puerto Rico's fiscal situation could directly impact millions of Americans in every state of the Union and the Commonwealth of Puerto Rico. Indeed, it is probable that more citizens invest in Puerto Rico bonds than still live in Puerto Rico.

Finally, it is important to remember that many Puerto Ricans invest in Puerto Rican bonds. We estimate that $15 billion of Puerto Rico bonds were purchased by Puerto Ricans. These are Puerto Rico's own hardworking citizens who pay Puerto Rico taxes [7]—or they are former residents of Puerto Rico who have moved to the mainland and depend on the bonds of their native Commonwealth for income.

These Puerto Rican investors, like mainland investors, bought their bonds after Puerto Rico was excluded from Chapter 9.

It is these on-island and mainland investors whose money has gone to build and operate Puerto Rico's firehouses, police stations, schools, sewer and water systems, highways, convention center and electrical plants. It is these investors, on-island and mainland, who have been champions of Puerto Rico and have interests that align with those of the people of Puerto Rico in seeing the Commonwealth thrive over the long-run.

And it is these individual, retail investors who Puerto Rico needs. Puerto Rico needed their investment in the past and Puerto Rico will need their investment in the future. Puerto Rico needs to raise billions of dollars for new electrical plants to meet air pollution regulations, for new water lines to avoid droughts in San Juan, for new sewer lines to meet water quality requirements, for maintenance of highways and bridges, for ordinary short term financing that every government needs to finance expenses between one tax collection cycle and the next.

A municipality that forces a restructuring on its bondholders will be locked out of the market for low-cost investment grade municipal bonds.[8] Thus, harming Puerto Rico's investor base as part of a restructuring will only make Puerto Rico's recovery harder, if not impossible, by shutting Puerto Rico out of the normal low-cost investment grade municipal bond market. It will leave Puerto Rico no recourse except to lenders who charge extraordinarily high rates to compensate for risk, or—in the end—the U.S. Treasury. It will also have a negative effect on the value of the $15 billion in Puerto Rico debt owned by on-island investors, leading to less money spent in the economy.

The only way to assure the Main Street retail investors who have entrusted their savings to Puerto Rico in the past that they can do so in the future is the creation of a strong, independent and federally appointed Authority.

THE PROBLEM TO BE SOLVED

The Commonwealth blames its problems on the individual retail investors who trusted the Commonwealth with their money. We submit that the Commonwealth created its own problems through over-optimistic revenue forecasting when budgeting, an economy with too much government and too little private enterprise, and poor management of public resources.

Consider:

- KPMG, the Commonwealth's own consultant, estimates that the Commonwealth could have obtained an additional $2.5 billion in revenue each year by improving tax collections and simplifying its tax structure.[9] This problem, again, is not new—it was highlighted in a 2006 report by the Brookings Institution.[10]

---

[7] As discussed below, Puerto Ricans do not pay Federal income tax, but they do pay the Federal Insurance Contributions Act tax.

[8] See, e.g., Ratings Methodology: U.S. Local Government General Obligation Debt, MOODY'S INVESTORS SERVICE 21 (Jan. 15, 2014) (considering defaults or "government's willingness and/or ability to meet financial obligations" as a factor in methodology for rating U.S. local government general obligation debt).

[9] See excerpts from KPMG, Unified Tax Code of Puerto Rico: Tax Policy Implementation Options Executive Summary (Oct. 31, 2014), available at http://www.hacienda.gobierno.pr/sites/default/files/unified_tax_code_of_pr_executive_summary_0.pdf (attached hereto as Exhibit B) (hereinafter the "KPMG Report").

[10] James Alm, Assessing Puerto Rico's Fiscal Policies, in RESTORING GROWTH IN PUERTO RICO: OVERVIEW AND POLICY OPTIONS 71 (Susan M. Collins et al. eds. 2006) (hereinafter "RESTORING GROWTH IN PUERTO RICO").

- KPMG likewise reports that the Commonwealth collects only 56 percent of its sales and use taxes.[11]
- The Commonwealth's funding gap is in material part due to municipal subsidies. These are required because municipalities base their property taxes on assessed valuations *from the 1950s*.[12]
- The Commonwealth has failed to file audited financial statements for 2 years.

Similar problems arise at the level of governmental corporations. The Puerto Rico Electric Power Authority, or PREPA, provides the best example.

- PREPA bills governmental corporations for power but historically has not collected what it is owed.[13]
- PREPA allows private customer bills to go unpaid for months before shutoff—and then instantly re-connects on payment without an adequate security deposit, effectively giving its customers months and months of credit. As of January 2015, PREPA suffered a 6 percent theft rate—the highest of any utility in the United States.[14]
- PREPA's current labor contract allows employees to get a year's pay for 9 months of work, and an employee earns overtime for more than 8 hours on any day even if the employee works less than 40 hours a week.[15]
- PREPA's 200 top managers are politically appointed and change with every administration.[16]
- According to publicly filed contracts, PREPA plans to dramatically over-pay for solar and wind—buying such power at an average cost of about 17 cents per KwH,[17] greatly in excess of PREPA's average cost of producing additional power at 11.33 cents per KwH in 2016[18] and *double* the 8.6 cents which Lazard estimates is the levelized cost of utility-scale solar power nationwide.[19]

These facts illuminate why PREPA is a poster child for the creation of a strong Authority. First, a strong authority could provide a credible assessment of PREPA's financial condition that could provide the basis for reforms. Second, a strong authority could enact the reforms that so far the Commonwealth and its municipalities have refused to adopt.

A STRONG AUTHORITY CAN FIX THESE PROBLEMS

In light of the Puerto Rico government's inability to manage its profound fiscal and operational problems, Congress should consider establishing an Authority for Puerto Rico based on what Congress did with a control board for the District of

[11]*See* excerpts from *KPMG Report*, supra note 9 (attached hereto as Exhibit B).
[12]Anne O. Krueger, et al., *Puerto Rico—A Way Forward*, 20 (July 13, 2015), *available at* http://www.bgfpr.com/documents/FinalUpdatedReport7-13-15.pdf (hereinafter "*Krueger Report*").
[13]*Accounts Receivable and CILT Report*, FTI Capital Advisors, LLC, 16 (Nov. 15, 2014), http://www.aeepr.com/Docs/restructuracion/PREPA%20AR%20and%20CILT%20Report%20Final.pdf.
[14]*Id.* at 45, 49; Siemens PTI Report Number R054–15, Integrated Resource Plan, Addendum I: Losses Considerations (July 15, 2015), *available at* http://www.aeepr.com/Docs/Ley57/PREPA%20IRP%20Addendum%20I%20%E2%80%93%20Draft%20for%20PREC%20review%20-%20July%207-2015%20-%20Losses%20Consideration.pdf.
[15]*Krueger Report*, supra note 12, at 18; Collective Bargaining Agreement Between PREPA and the Union of Electrical and Irrigation Industry Workers of Puerto Rico (Aug. 24, 2008), *available at* http://www.utier.org/Contenido/CONVENIOFINALWEB.pdf. Employees receive 30 paid vacation days, 19 paid sick days and 20 paid holidays, for a total of 69 paid days off each year. *Id.* Assuming there are 260 working days in a year, PREPA employees accrue paid time for approximately 25%, or about 3 months, of each year. Unused vacation days can be carried over for a year; sick days can be accumulated and carried over from year to year without limit. *Id.*
[16]*Hearing Before the Puerto Rico Senate Committee on Energy Matters and Water Resources* (Apr. 14, 2015) (Testimony of Lisa Donahue, Chief Restructuring Officer of PREPA).
[17]C. Kunkel et al., *Opportunity for a New Direction for Puerto Rico's Electric System*, INSTITUTE FOR ENERGY ECONOMICS AND FINANCIAL ANALYSIS (Sept. 10, 2015), *available at* http://ieefa.org/wp-content/uploads/2015/09/Opportunity-for-A-New-Direction-for-Puerto-Ricos-Electric-System-Sept-10-2015.pdf.
[18]*See* PREPA, *PREPA's Transformation: A Path to Sustainability*, 9, as set forth in *PREPA Public Disclosure* (July 22, 2015), *available at* http://emma.msrb.org/ER906457-ER708173-ER1109700.pdf. PREPA's July 2015 report estimated the 11.33 cents cost of buying additional power based on current and currently projected natural gas and oil prices. The IEEFA's September 2015 Report, although issued 2 months later, used 2014 natural gas and oil prices (more than twice as high) to support IEEFA's conclusion that renewable power is cheaper than conventional power.
[19]LAZARD, *Levelized Cost of Energy Analysis—Version 8.0*, 2 (2014), *available at* www.lazard.com/media/1777/levelized_cost_of_energy_-_version_80.pdf.

Columbia back in the 1990s, when the District of Columbia had its financial problems. Many observers agree that the control board which Congress created for the District of Columbia was instrumental in the District's dramatic revitalization that is evident today.

Moreover, I would note that, when Congress examined legislative proposals to help the District of Columbia in the 1990s, opting for a control board, it also considered permitting the District of Columbia to access Chapter 9—*but it expressly rejected that option* because it found that:

> **[T]he Bankruptcy Code as it stands is neither intended to nor designed to promote judicial restructuring of a municipal government that suffers chronic, structural budget deficits. . . . Unlike a Control Board, the [Bankruptcy] Court provides no mechanism for acquiring independent financial expertise services. Nor can it provide legally binding guidance to the debtor on administrative or structural reform.**[20]

If Congress were to create an Authority for Puerto Rico and also grant Chapter 9 for Puerto Rico, Chapter 9 would not only: (1) undermine the rule of law and result in a bailout of Puerto Rico on the backs of well over a million U.S. taxpayers throughout the mainland (and Puerto Rico) who are retail investors in Puerto Rico bonds, but also (2) undermine the reforms hoped to be achieved through an Authority, as Puerto Rico could simply repudiate its debts through bankruptcy, thereby alleviating the political imperative to implement tough reforms recommended by the Authority.

A strong Authority provides the best chance to fix the problems of Puerto Rico and its governmental corporations. The Authority should have a small number of board members—I suggest 5—because the smaller the board the stronger it will be.

A strong Authority must have board members from both Puerto Rico and the mainland that are acceptable to both Congress and Puerto Rico. The board should be bipartisan, appointed by the President and confirmed by the Senate, have experience in municipal finance and inspire the trust and confidence of Puerto Rico's creditors.

The board members will be asked to work long and hard on the problems of Puerto Rico. Their terms should be several years because Puerto Rico's problems will not be solved quickly. Further, board members should be compensated so that the Authority obtains the committed service of the most serious, experienced and best people—and Congress should seek out members who are preferably fluent in Puerto Rico's two official languages, English and Spanish, to help ensure effective communication with both Congress and the people of Puerto Rico.

The Authority should retain an executive director of unquestioned competence, stature and dedication, and the Authority should have the resources to hire committed, experienced, knowledgeable and bilingual financial professionals.

The powers of the Authority should be broad and must include the power of the purse, but they need not trespass on the sovereignty of the Commonwealth.

The U.S. Treasury already funds billions of dollars to Puerto Rico every year and the Commonwealth is asking for more—more Medicaid and Federal credit support. The continuation of, or increase in, any support from the Federal Government can be conditioned on the Authority's approval of the Commonwealth's budget on a yearly basis—just as the District of Columbia Control Board's approval was required for the District to have access to Federal funding.

With respect to the Commonwealth's government corporations, the Authority should have the same power that Michigan had over Detroit and has over its other cities: the appointment of a manager with power to hire, fire, reject and renegotiate contracts, revise work rules, and restructure pensions.[21]

A strong Authority can bring expenditures under control. I cite the financial problems and recovery of New York City in the mid to late 1970s as the largest example. New York's budget had ballooned in the 1960s and 1970s as government grew bigger and bigger.[22]

Only outside intervention brought New York City's budget under control. Everyone remembers New York State's imposition of the Municipal Assistance Corporation, which to this day ensures that the City keeps its books in accordance with Governmental Accounting Standards. Fewer people remember that the U.S.

---

[20] *District of Columbia Financial Responsibility and Management Assistance Act of 1995*, H.R. Rep. No. 104–96, at 17 (1995).

[21] *See generally* 2012 Mich. Pub. Act 436, the Local Financial Stability and Choice Act.

[22] *See* Exhibit C.

Treasury also exercised oversight over New York—there was a special office created in Washington to deal with New York City.[23]

The oversight was effective, its results well known. New York City brought its labor costs under control, cut the size of its government and set the stage for an economic recovery.

More recently, the District of Columbia Control Board, with Anthony Williams as chief financial officer and later mayor, brought the District from deficit and fiscal crisis to surplus in less than 2 years.[24]

The Authority's role should not be permanent. Just as with the District of Columbia Control Board, the Authority's control should expire upon a congressionally approved determination of success, which should include, among other factors, access to short and long term capital markets at reasonable rates, a balanced budget for a few years in a row, and audited, credible financial statements.

Only after maximum operational changes have been made and maximum operational savings have been achieved, and only if debt restructuring is still necessary, the manager could then have the power to negotiate and implement a restructuring with the *vote of two-thirds* of the debt to be restructured.

Finally, it is critical that neither the Authority nor Puerto Rico have the authority to authorize Chapter 9 filings because Chapter 9 in its current form allows municipal debtors to do as little possible by paying creditors as little as possible.

Chapter 9 used to give creditors a vote—indeed, prior to 1978, it required agreement by a majority of bonds to even begin a case[25]—but the 1978 statute reduced the vote to a formality. So long as a Chapter 9 plan has been accepted by one class of creditors, no matter how small, it can be confirmed over the objection of all other creditors, no matter how large or how many.[26]

Chapter 9's other requirements—that the plan be "fair and equitable," "not discriminate unfairly" and be "in the best interests of creditors"—provide little protection to creditors,[27] who do not even have the ability to propose their own plan.[28]

Once in Chapter 9, the Bankruptcy Code bars the court from ordering the municipality to do anything[29]—the municipality cannot be compelled to cut its costs, raise its revenues, collect its taxes, renegotiate its contracts, restructure its pensions, reform its budgets, anything. The only thing a court can do is dismiss the case.

So the argument often heard, that Chapter 9 "builds consensus," is fake. A municipality is free to make minimal operational changes, cut a deal with one favored class of creditors, and tell all other classes that their votes mean nothing. The only remedy that creditors have in Chapter 9, and the only power a court has with respect to the municipal debtor, is to get out of Chapter 9.

No matter how strong the Authority or its emergency managers, the availability of Chapter 9 or any compulsory debt restructuring reduces the incentive of any government to enact real reforms, will cut access to the capital markets and inevitably

---

[23] MARTIN SHEFTER, POLITICAL CRISIS FISCAL CRISIS: THE COLLAPSE AND REVIVAL OF NEW YORK CITY 134, 151 (Columbia Univ. Press Morningside ed. 1992).

[24] *See* ALICE RIVLIN, ET AL., BUILDING THE BEST CAPITAL CITY IN THE WORLD, A REPORT BY DC APPLESEED AND OUR NATION'S CAPITAL 109 (2008), http://www.brookings.edu/~/media/Research/Files/Reports/2008/12/18-dc-revitalization-garrison-rivlin/appendix.pdf (hereinafter the "BROOKINGS REPORT") (attached hereto as Exhibit D).

[25] Section 83(a) of the Bankruptcy Act of 1898, *as amended by* The Municipal Bankruptcy Act of 1937, Pub. L. No. 302, 50 Stat. 652 (1937) (codified at 11 U.S.C. § 403(a) (1970)).

[26] 11 U.S.C. § 901(a) (incorporating § 1129(a)(10)). Chapter 9 also allows debtors to classify disparate creditors together, even if the results will be inequitable. In Stockton's bankruptcy case, unsecured bond claims were classified with the much larger retiree medical claims, even though retiree medical claimants could also look to a spouse's insurance, the Affordable Care Act, and their pension claims, which were being paid in full. *See In re City of Stockton, Cal.*, 526 B.R. 35, 62 (Bankr. E.D. Cal. 2015) *aff'd in part, dismissed in part*, 542 B.R. 261 (B.A.P. 9th Cir. 2015).

[27] In Detroit's bankruptcy case, *In re City of Detroit, Mich.*, 524 B.R. 147 (Bankr. E.D. Mich. 2014), Bankruptcy Judge Rhodes held that paying one group of bondholders 13 cents while pensioners received 59–60 cents was not "unfair discrimination" because it did not offend "the judgment of conscience," including "the Court's experience and sense of morality." This standard—which had never before been applied to "unfair discrimination"—allowed the court to confirm the plan irrespective of the bondholder vote. *Id.* at 253, 256–58.

The "best interests of creditors" test also does little to protect creditors. In the Detroit case, Judge Rhodes further held that the plan was in the best interests of creditors because bondholder remedies would not yield a better result outside of bankruptcy. *City of Detroit*, 524 B.R. at 213–17. Precedent under old Chapter IX required a municipality to do what it could to pay creditors. *See Fano v. Newport Heights Irrigation District*, 114 F.2d 563, 565–66 (9th Cir. 1940).

[28] 11 U.S.C. § 941.

[29] 11 U.S.C. §§ 903–904.

lead the Commonwealth and its governmental corporations returning to Congress for financial support.[30]

CHAPTER 9 WOULD HINDER, NOT HELP, THE AUTHORITY

A comparison of the District of Columbia (which had a control board but no access to bankruptcy via Chapter 9), with Jefferson County, Alabama (Chapter 9, no control board) and the city of Detroit (Chapter 9, 18-month emergency manager[31]) shows why a strong control board is required and why Chapter 9 is an impediment to required reform.

The District of Columbia Control Board closed D.C. General Hospital over the objections of the D.C. City Council because the District had to cover deficits of $90 million—and because a local system of clinics and hospitals could provide better and less expensive medical care for residents.

By contrast, there was no control board for Jefferson County, Alabama. Jefferson County's Cooper-Green Medical Center was costing the county $10 million a year to employ over 528 staff with fewer than 38 patients, even though it had 100 available beds.[32] The world-class University of Alabama/Birmingham Hospital is literally across the street with capacity to take Cooper-Green's patients. It took years—including 2 years in Chapter 9—for the County Commissioners to transition Cooper Green to an urgent care clinic.[33]

Detroit had similar problems when it resorted to Chapter 9.

Kevyn Orr, the emergency manager appointed by Governor Snyder, had an 18-month term to solve a range of problems.[34] Orr cut debt service and moved retiree medical benefits off the City's budget and onto the Federal Government through the Affordable Care Act, but he made minimal cuts to pension—zero reduction in current benefits for police and fire,[35] a 4.5 percent cut for general employees,[36] and he allowed the City to adopt some of the same questionable practices that led to pension underfunding in the first place.

Detroit's pension problems are far from solved. Detroit's plan put in place a 10-year moratorium on pension funding, but Detroit must make yearly payments thereafter. Recent projections show that the balloon payment due in 2024 has risen to $195 million, approximately 71 percent higher than the $114 million originally projected.[37] Even former Bankruptcy Judge Rhodes, now a consultant to the Puerto Rico government, who confirmed the City's plan of adjustment, has admitted that Detroit's bankruptcy was a "missed opportunity" for greater pension reform.[38]

Lingering pension issues are one of many reasons that even now, over a year after Detroit emerged from bankruptcy, Detroit has no access to the low-cost ordinary municipal market. Detroit as an issuer still has a junk credit rating. Its new unsecured notes, issued under its bankruptcy plan, trade at around 23 cents on the dollar. Following its bankruptcy, Detroit has been able to access the credit markets only through secured debt issued by a State of Michigan entity secured by income

---

[30] Some witnesses have predicted that governmental corporations can obtain "debtor in possession" or "DIP" financing in a Chapter 9 bankruptcy case. There is no basis for this prediction. No private sector lender makes a DIP unless secured by a first lien on collateral. The government corporations cannot grant such a lien because most of them have already pledged all their collateral to existing bondholders. Therefore, if Puerto Rico's government corporations were given access to Chapter 9, any bankruptcy case would be like General Motors and Chrysler—the only entity that would provide DIP financing would be the U.S. Government.

[31] The statute providing for the appointment of Detroit's emergency manager gave the manager a term of 18 months.

[32] *See* Barnett Wright, *Dr. Sandral Hullett of Cooper Green Hospital, Among 210 Who Received Lay Off Notices*, THE BIRMINGHAM NEWS (Dec. 20, 2012), http://blog.al.com/spotnews/2012/dr_sandral_hullett_ceo_of_coop.html; B. Wright, *Cooper Green Ending Inpatient, Emergency Room Services*, THE BIRMINGHAM NEWS (Dec. 12, 2012), http://blog.al.com/spotnews/2012/12cooper_green_mercy_hospital_to_2.html.

[33] *Id.*

[34] Mr. Orr ended up serving as Detroit's emergency manager from his appointment on March 2013 until Detroit emerged from bankruptcy in December 2014. Della Cassia, *Emergency Manager Kevyn Orr Steps Down as Detroit Emerges From Bankruptcy*, PBS Newshour (Dec. 12, 2014), http://www.pbs.org/newshour/rundown/emergency-manager-kevyn-orr-steps-detroit-emerges-bankruptcy.

[35] The cost of living adjustment was eliminated for police and fire retirees.

[36] Chris Christoff, *Detroit Pension Cuts from Bankruptcy Prompt Cries of Betrayal*, BLOOMBERG (Feb. 2, 2015), http://www.bloomberg.com/news/articles/2015-02-05/detroit-pension-cuts-from-bankruptcy-prompt-cries-of-betrayal.

[37] *See* Matthew Dolan et al., *$195M pension payment might derail Detroit's Recovery*, DETROIT FREE PRESS (Nov. 15, 2015), http://www.freep.com/story/news/local/detroit-bankruptcy/2015/11/14/detroit-pension-balloon-payment-estimated-195m/75657200.

[38] *Id.*

tax revenues that the City never touches.[39] Puerto Rico has no entity to enable it to access the credit markets other than the U.S. Treasury.

By contrast, the D.C. Control Board was able to restore the District's access to the markets. By 2001, all three major rating agencies deemed the District's bonds investment grade.[40] One of my clients, Franklin Advisers, was an early investor in bonds issued by the District under the Control Board. Standard & Poor's now rates the District at AA—several notches above investment grade.

Orr made no structural changes to the Detroit government. The City exited Chapter 9 with the same 28 government agencies it had when it entered bankruptcy.[41] Note that Puerto Rico has at least 120 government agencies and 78 municipalities for an island with 3.5 million people.[42]

By contrast, Mayor Anthony Williams and the D.C. Control Board focused on reducing government, collecting (not raising) taxes and attracting private sector employers to the District. The comparison of the District of Columbia with Puerto Rico is instructive. Puerto Rico's collection rates are extremely low:

> Some analysts estimate that uncollected personal income taxes amounted to 29.7 percent of actual income tax revenues in 1987 and 24.9 percent of tax revenues in 1992.[43]

The District recognized the importance of improving collections as a fundamental part of its turnaround:

> In addition to strictly managing expenditures, the District's growth in revenue generation since FY 1997 is a striking success. Total tax revenue grew by 92 percent and gross revenues increased almost 53 percent from FY 1997 to 2007. The District took three important steps to make this possible: (1) DC made improvements to its current revenue collection capacity; (2) it improved its overall financial health, and, thus, its capacity to generate revenue, especially through the real estate market; and (3) it developed cautious estimates of future revenues.[44]

The contrasting experiences of Detroit and DC provide valuable instruction on the benefits of employing a strong control board to address the Commonwealth's problem and the dangers of resorting to Chapter 9.

CONCLUSION

Puerto Rico's problem in a nutshell is that its private sector employs too low a percentage of working-age citizens, its public resources are mismanaged and its government employs too great a percentage of its working-age citizens. The Commonwealth's cry of "humanitarian crisis" is nothing more than a plea for third parties—bondholders through cuts to debt service, the Federal Government through loans, grants or subsidies—to maintain the size of an un-maintainable and poorly managed government, to fund the patient's illness, not to cure it.

If Puerto Rico is to survive and flourish, it must create an island economy where the private sector generates income for its citizens and supports its own government. Supporting or increasing government expenditures will not work. Cutting debt service to maintain government spending will not work. A strong Authority which reduces government, enhances management of public resources and supports the private sector has a chance of doing so—as it did in DC and New York City.

---

[39] *See* Michigan Finance Authority Offering Memorandum for Local Government Loan Program Revenue Bonds, Series 2014F (City of Detroit Financial Recovery Income Tax Revenue and Refunding Local Project Bonds) (Dec. 10, 2014).

[40] D.C.'s general obligation bonds were rated below investment grade in 1995; starting in 1998, as a result of the District's financial turnaround, the rating agencies began steadily increasing the ratings. *See* U.S. General Accounting Office, Testimony Before the Subcommittee on the District of Columbia, Committee on Government Reform, House of Representatives and Subcommittee on Oversight of Government Management, Restructuring and the District of Columbia, Committee on Governmental Affairs, U.S. Senate, "District of Columbia: Oversight in the Post-Control Board Period" 6 (June 8, 2001), http://www.gao.gov/assets/110/108870.pdf.

[41] *City of Detroit—Expert Witness Report of Stephen J. Spencer* (July 2014).

[42] *Annual Estimates of the Resident Population: April 1, 2010 to July 1, 2015*, U.S. CENSUS BUREAU (Jan. 22, 2016, 10:15 PM), http://factfinder.census.gov/faces/tableservices/jsf/pages/productview.xhtml?pid=PEP_2014_PEPANNRES&src=pt; *Agency Directory*, PR.GOV (Jan. 24, 2016, 12:30 PM), http://www2.pr.gov/Directorios/ Pages/DirectoriodeAgencias.aspx; Steven J. Davis & Luis A. Rivera-Batiz, *The Climate for Business Development and Employment Growth*, in RESTORING GROWTH IN PUERTO RICO, supra note 10, at 57.

[43] James Alm, *Assessing Puerto Rico's Fiscal Policies*, in RESTORING GROWTH IN PUERTO RICO, supra note 10, at 71.

[44] THE BROOKINGS REPORT, supra note 24, at 113.

Any other solution leads the Commonwealth, as it led General Motors and Chrysler, back to the Federal Government for cash the private markets will no longer supply. In addition to eliminating access to private markets, access to Chapter 9 would hurt individual investors—the very people who were willing to invest in Puerto Rico's infrastructure and development in the first place.

**

[Attachments to Mr. Mayer's Prepared Statement (Exhibits A–D) are not included in the printed hearing. These documents are included in the hearing record and are being retained in the Committee's official files.]

———

Mr. YOUNG. Thank you, sir. I listened to your proposal on the heel of the Ranking Member. You said one word that disturbs me a great deal, the appointment of the control board confirmed by the Senate. Let's forget that part because it will never happen. I'm serious about that. I watched this. So, we will eliminate that word. That is a dark hole.

Mr. MAYER. Mr. Chairman, I apologize. I am really far more focused on making sure the control board has the quality people that it needs than how——

Mr. YOUNG. You will have it confirmed by the House. How's that? That would be a lot better.

Mr. MAYER. Yes, Mr. Chairman.

Mr. YOUNG. Mr. Pierluisi.

Mr. PIERLUISI. Thank you, Chairman. I am going to try to lay out a couple of facts that I believe are beyond dispute, or at the very least are supported by the vast majority of my constituents.

The first one is that Puerto Rico is facing a very serious, unprecedented liquidity crisis. There are payments in the immediate horizon that, for all intents and purposes, unless the government of Puerto Rico obtains adequate access to the markets, the government is going to fail in making it. You are going to have massive defaults starting possibly in May of this year, in all likelihood in July of this year. And that is not good for anybody. It is not good for creditors. It is not good for the people of Puerto Rico. It is not good for Congress. It is not good for the municipal markets, and I can go on. So, we need to deal with that.

Another fact, the budgeting system of the government of Puerto Rico, the accounting system, the financial reporting system, leaves a lot to be desired. It needs to be reformed drastically. Everybody agrees.

Third uncontested fact, the amount of public debt in Puerto Rico equals Puerto Rico's GNP. By any measure, that is a lot of debt. And Puerto Rico has not been growing significantly ever since 8 or 9 years ago. So, that is the scenario.

With that scenario in mind, I tell you, Mayor Williams, I believe that the majority of people of Puerto Rico support the concept of a Federal oversight board assisting Puerto Rico in putting our fiscal house in order within reason. But the board itself is not going to be a solution. You also need to provide Puerto Rico with either better treatment in Federal programs or otherwise access to the financial markets so that we do not fail to comply with our obligations in the markets. That is the challenge that we should address here and I hope that you can comment on that.

Last, and let me be specific about a couple of examples: DC, the way that the Medicaid programs work in the states, the Federal Government provides a substantial amount of the funding. In the case of DC, the Federal Government was giving you 50 percent, Mayor Williams. You know that. Then as a result of the Revitalization Act, which was part of the legislative package, the Congress increased it to 70 percent, and it assisted DC.

Professor Johnson mentions the EITC program, earned income tax credit program, which is the best anti-poverty program in the states. In Puerto Rico, we have an extremely low labor participation rate. We need to create jobs, get the people to work in the formal economy. That would be a great tool. I will leave it at that. I would like both of you to comment on specific measures apart from instituting a board that could assist Puerto Rico in getting into a path toward recovery.

Mr. WILLIAMS. I think the entity in Washington, DC was able to do something very important, and that, I think, was to begin establishing an environment of success, a climate for investment, very importantly for citizens and investors. I think these issues about migration, it created an environment for investment where people wanted to invest, again, where they wanted to live. How was that done? Create reliable financial information. Create reliable government financial operations.

Before you ask for anything, make sure you are collecting, not only collecting your revenue, but cashing your checks. We had checks in bundles on a floor in a room. We were not even cashing checks. So cash your checks, collect your revenue, manage your government operations, create settled expectations.

Begin bringing down the size of government. Not that the size of government alone is a solution, but how can you create confidence unless you are addressing fundamental governmental operations. Building on that and on that basis, then you are looking at your balance sheet and you are saying, "OK, on the basis of all this, we are collecting the revenue we can, we have reduced government operations. You know what? We still need to look at our relationship with the Federal Government." I think that ought to be the approach here. Look at restructuring debt, look at the relationship with the Federal Government, look at these things after you have put the basic housekeeping in order. And while you are doing that, you certainly need liquidity, but that is different to me than doing the Chapter 9 kind of solution in Detroit.

Mr. YOUNG. I am going to let Professor Johnson comment for 1 minute. He used most of his time up giving a great presentation, but I will let Mr. Johnson have 1 minute. Start that time over.

Mr. JOHNSON. Thank you, Mr. Chairman. Yes, these programs were exactly what I had in mind when I agreed with you at the beginning. If Puerto Rico were a state, we would not have the same crisis today. The cap on Medicaid for Puerto Rico, which does not exist for the states; EITC, absolutely a very important program for states with lots of poor people, not available at all to Puerto Rico; and the child tax credit as well, Mr. Pierluisi, which you have proposed to extend to Puerto Rico. Again, it makes complete sense.

Now, this would change the terms of the financial relationship between Puerto Rico and the Federal Government and it would be taking on some additional obligations for the Federal Government. I understand that, too.

I think there are two reasons to consider this, one is you treated Puerto Rico more like a state, and that is how Puerto Rico should be treated in this fiscal relationship.

The second thing is in the historical precedence that we have including, particularly, DC. My understanding as a DC taxpayer is that the relationship between the Federal Government and the DC government changed in terms of what the Federal Government was responsible for. Those terms were adjusted in favor of DC, and I think it is that adjustment that would be very helpful and appropriate to Puerto Rico right now.

Mr. YOUNG. Thank you. And with that, Mr. Labrador.

Mr. Labrador, would you like—you are not a member of the subcommittee, but you are welcome to go ahead, especially when you start mimicking me. I really appreciate it.

Mr. LABRADOR. I am trying to be as handsome as you are.

Mr. YOUNG. Well, oh—do you want 10 minutes? No, go ahead.

Mr. LABRADOR. Thank you, Mr. Chairman. Thank you, Mr. Pierluisi. Thank you everyone, and especially the witnesses for being here. This is a very important issue. I happen to serve on both committees that are dealing with this issue. I am serving in the Judiciary Committee, where we will be looking at the bankruptcy issue; and I am serving in this committee, where we are looking at the oversight board.

I really appreciate the work that has been done by a lot of people. At the Energy and Mineral Resources Subcommittee's hearing last month, I made the point that nothing said at the hearing or elsewhere should really be interpreted as encouraging the government of Puerto Rico to delay any kind of actions that they need to do right now. I think there are some things that they should be doing right now that will help us in our understanding of where they want to go with this fiscal situation. I think that is important for them.

I had the great privilege of meeting with the Speaker of the House of Puerto Rico, and we had a really fantastic conversation about what they are trying to do, and I am encouraging them to take some steps right now before we even decide in Congress what we are going to be doing.

I have a couple of questions for you, Mr. Williams, and I appreciate your vast experience in dealing with this. I wonder if you could comment on what Mr. Moers Mayer—I think I am saying your name correctly—what he said about the financial—he talked about the difference between Detroit and Washington, DC, and he said that you guys did not—and I hope I understood this correctly—you guys did not have Chapter 9. All you had was the oversight board.

And he talked about the difference in the result of what happened with Chapter 9 where Detroit now is still financially unstable, but it seems like Washington, DC is doing much better. Could you please speak to those comments that he made?

Mr. WILLIAMS. Timing is of the essence, but I think it is important to build confidence, create these expectations I am talking about before you ask for incentives, however they are warranted by past experience, and they certainly were warranted in DC, before you ask for additional changes in relationship with the Federal Government.

A great example would be Medicaid. We did not really get the Medicaid change until I was Mayor, and it was based on the confidence we had built in reforming the government that the House and the Senate Appropriation Committees finally gave us a 70/30 versus a 50/50 Medicaid. And, likewise with the Revitalization Act and the spinoff of a number of things that our government was doing that we should not have been doing.

If we had tried to do that at the beginning with the lack of confidence we had, I think it would have been a nonstarter. So, I think these things are essential, this relationship with the Federal Government is essential, but you have to create a climate of confidence, settled expectations before you can begin to look at these larger issues.

Mr. LABRADOR. I think you are hitting my point exactly, because I understand that we need a financial control board. I am undecided about the bankruptcy, but I am open to it. I am open to the bankruptcy protections, but it seems to me that bankruptcy is not a plan. Bankruptcy is a step in a plan. And I am not sure where that bankruptcy protection should come in, if at all.

Mr. Carlos Garcia, could you speak to that issue a little bit and specifically to what Mr. Williams is saying that the government of Puerto Rico needs to build, and I agree with him 100 percent, the confidence that they are moving forward with the appropriate plan.

Mr. GARCIA. I agree with that, and that is the reason why I shared some of our experience when we had the control board from 2009, 2011, and that was the first point, being able to establish the confidence of all the stakeholders. It was not only the bondholders, but it was everybody and all the constituents. It was a lot of hard work, but by doing that hard work, it is what gains the confidence of everybody else to be able to manage all the other issues.

In regards to the restructuring mechanisms, I mean I agree it is a tool. But right now, the consequences and the issues of Puerto Rico, it is not only solving a very complicated fiscal situation, but it is trying to find a path that finally provides the opportunity for Puerto Rico to be able to grow, so we don't have to be dealing with this again in 2 years, in 5 years, or 10 years. So, it has to be a comprehensive solution. As I mentioned in my testimony, it has to do a lot with the loss of an economic model in Puerto Rico if you are not able to combine those two measures.

And finally, if you do not provide a single resolution mechanism that allows them to be able to balance the equities, as I mentioned, the formal debts are very important, but all the other compromise and commitments that Puerto Rico had made to their pensioners, to health, and to the well-being of Puerto Rico need to be balanced. And I think that doing it through the authority in combination with all other powers will be the best way to go at this time.

Mr. LABRADOR. Thank you. And, Mr. Moers Mayer, if the people of Puerto Rico and the government of Puerto Rico do all the things that are necessary to gain that financial stability and to gain that financial confidence, and we still see that the bankruptcy should be a step in the process, why would you be opposed to that?

Mr. MAYER. Thank you for asking that question. All we want is the vote. We want the ability to vote on a restructuring plan for the governmental corporations, and it is important to mention again. When we talk about the crisis, and we talk about healthcare, and when we talk about payments of pensions, you are always talking about obligations of the Commonwealth of Puerto Rico itself with respect to which Chapter 9 simply would not apply. And if Puerto Rico were a state, Chapter 9 would definitely not apply, and there might even be constitutional issues as to whether or not Chapter 9 could apply.

So, you are only talking about governmental corporations. You are talking about the electric company, the sewer company, and the highway company. And, yes, we think an authority could provide solutions to the operating problems of those authorities. And when it does, our people would be prepared to vote by the right majorities to do a deal. We did that in the Puerto Rican Electric Power Authority, and the model for that is apparently acceptable enough that legislators in Puerto Rico are thinking about applying it to the sewer authority.

So, you have a limited number of government corporations that are in the process of working this out. And would we accept a majority rules clause with respect to that corporate debt? Yes, we would, after the improvements had been made.

Mr. LABRADOR. OK. Thank you. My time has expired.

Mr. YOUNG. Thank you, sir. The Ranking Member of the Full Committee, Mr. Grijalva.

Mr. GRIJALVA. Thank you very much, Mr. Chairman. And when you were admonishing the person with the white hair for bopping up and down, I was glad it was not Chairman Bishop that you were looking at at that point.

Mr. YOUNG. I was looking to my left.

Mr. GRIJALVA. We were both relieved. The debt crisis in Puerto Rico, Mr. Chairman, is a major part of the problem we are facing, which makes to some extent the comparisons to DC a little off. In fact, I don't think it is the right comparison.

When we talk about control boards, unbridled full control boards, answerable to no constituency or other elected officials being made irrelevant in the process and other specific organizations participating, I think we should probably be comparing Puerto Rico in that absolute sense to Flint, Michigan, where austerity, as the main vehicle for balancing books and bringing things into line, has produced the crisis that we see now with lead poisoning.

I think the definition of what we mean by oversight is critical in any legislation, and I think that the issue of all the stakeholders being part of the process is fine with me, but I think there is humanity involved here, and that has to be taken into account.

I wanted to ask you, Mr. LeCompte, Bloomberg Government recently released an analysis of lobbying data and found that in the second and third quarter of 2015 alone over $47 million was spent lobbying on Puerto Rican issues. The numbers give you some idea as to the scale of profit at stake here. The business of spending this much money on lobbying—see their level of spending on lobbying as a worthwhile investment toward profits, which means they are probably significantly bigger.

A dollar that goes into that process to hedge funds, other investors being the first in line, is a dollar that does not go to schools, nurses, police, and fire protection. You mention austerity that has already visited the families of Puerto Rico. Can you expand on what it looks like day to day without any mechanism for restructuring and without any oversight mechanism that still respects the citizens?

Mr. LeCompte. Congressman Grijalva, the situation on the ground is absolutely grave. Working with the religious leaders and the religious institutions that are really on the front lines of dealing with the crisis, where nearly one out of two people already live in poverty, we are seeing daily self-imposed austerity continue on the island.

The most recent being that special ed teachers had their salaries cut, greater cuts to healthcare on the island. It is absolutely desperate. I think it is also important because I certainly agree with my colleagues on the panel and the different viewpoints that have been lifted by the various members of the committee.

The creditors themselves are a diverse group. The religious institutions that we represent, the catholic church, all of the mainline protestant groups in Puerto Rico, are creditors. The various unions in Puerto Rico are creditors. These are groups that own Puerto Rico bonds and have substantial commitments. At the same time, they understand very clearly that there needs to be haircut to get the debt back to sustainable levels.

I think in terms of the lobbying issues that you have raised, there are many creditors that have very legitimate stakes and want a resolution that makes the most sense to benefit the people of Puerto Rico, and also to be able to get some economic growth back behind their investment. But I think there is a small group of investors that is trying to prevent any kind of process from moving forward, and I think that group does not care about the austerity that is continuing. They just care about getting paid.

Mr. GRIJALVA. Thank you. Mr. Johnson, there is a consensus that Puerto Rico's capacity to repay its debt ultimately depends on restoring economic growth on the island and that there can be no economic recovery without significant restructuring of the debt. While I am aware that there are negotiations ongoing between the government of Puerto Rico and its creditors on an agreement to restructuring the debt, wouldn't a process, such as Chapter 9 or some other similar regimen, be a more effective way to obtain true debt restructuring rather than a voluntary agreement where all sides could walk away at any time?

Mr. JOHNSON. Congressman, that is absolutely a key question to be asking today. And I would emphasize, there is a continuum of choices for Congress to make. On the one hand, you could choose to allow bankruptcy, the Chapter 9 which had already been discussed. On the other hand, you could prefer to leave it entirely as a voluntary process, which is hard. There are also some intermediate approaches, and I think this is why having a growth authority approach is a very good one.

The growth authority could have the ability to negotiate these deals and, subject to some voting and if the creditors are willing to be reasonable, that is absolutely the best way forward subject to being able to get growth back, which is important for the creditors as well as for all the citizens of Puerto Rico.

In the intermediate case, you probably do need permission—you need some sort of arrangement where a court would approve, let's say, a prepackaged restructuring in order to prevent a relatively few creditors from holding out. Now what Mr. Mayer was talking about with the majority voting, typically if you have a majority, then the holdouts have to surrender their debt on the same terms.

So, I think you want to think comprehensively, and what I am also talking about with the intermediate solution is not just the municipal debt, not just the debt that sometimes you will talk about that could be under Chapter 9 if this were a state—I am suggesting that all of the obligations, all Puerto Rico be reviewed and assessed by this growth authority with a view to restructuring that is fair and equitable, does not treat all creditors the same way, because there are different classes of creditors, but all of the debt should be included in that assessment that will be delegated presumably to the authority with the backing of the court system.

Mr. MAYER. But it is important to note that such authority has never been granted to any state in the Union. If you want Puerto Rico to be treated like a state, then you have to treat the obligations of the Commonwealth as you would treat the state obligations.

Mr. JOHNSON. Yes, you cannot grant this to a state. Puerto Rico is not a state, and it is not being treated like a state.

Mr. YOUNG. Mr. Johnson, please.

Mr. Ruiz.

Mr. RUIZ. Thank you, Mr. Chairman. Puerto Rico is part of our Nation, and we have a responsibility to the Puerto Rican people to provide them with the tools and opportunities to achieve the American dream. It is nearly undisputable at this point that Puerto Rico is faced with a debt crisis, a crisis that if we fail to address will break our promise to the Puerto Rican people, to our fellow American citizens.

I appreciate that this hearing has been convened to explore how we can become part of the solution and what pragmatic steps should be taken to empower Puerto Rico to succeed. I also want to remind everybody that a budget is a reflection of our values and that people are more than a spreadsheet. Numbers in that spreadsheet have a story and they have lives.

We want to set up the restructuring process to help set up Puerto Rico to succeed. In most of these committees and counsels that have financial responsibility and advice, there is a lot of cutting, there are a lot of austerity measures that do not really deal with the growth of a community such as Puerto Rico. So, the things that we want for growth include the education, the workforce development, the infrastructure development, job training, and also healthcare.

How will those factors play into a committee such as the one we are thinking of, the board? Anybody?

Mr. WILLIAMS. I think the right kind of entity can create a level of confidence where economic incentives begin to work, where the right restructuring of government begins to feed into that—basically turning a vicious cycle into a virtuous cycle, creating economic investment. And I would respectfully disagree with the Congressman—I think the experience in DC, the experience in Philadelphia, the experience in New York, the experience in Cleveland with then-Mayor Voinovich, is that the right kind of leadership with the right control entity can not only right-size a government, if you will, but as everyone is saying and most importantly, begin to create a climate for economic investment and growth.

Mr. RUIZ. Well, I don't think there was any disagreement in that statement, because I think the counsel can do both or the board can do both, and that was my point.

Professor Johnson?

Mr. JOHNSON. Congressman, if you take the example of the cost of energy in Puerto Rico, I think this is very important, it is expensive, and it is much more expensive, for example, than in Florida, in part because the plant used is out of date and they do not use natural gas, for example, that would be considerably cheaper. So, this is a sector that is crying out for investment. It is essential to all parts of the economy. You are not going to get investment in that sector unless you sort out the debt overhang issue.

And going forward, presumably there is a role for some public sector, but also the private sector. I think the Chairman, again, put his finger on it at the beginning when he said you want to create an environment for investment, and that is what Mr. Williams is saying as well——

Mr. MAYER. Thank you. With respect to Professor Johnson, there is a deal to create that investment. We have spent 18 months negotiating it.

Mr. RUIZ. Thank you very much. This is my last question to Mr. LeCompte. Self-empowerment is very important to the people of Puerto Rico. It is very important to me. How can we incorporate citizen participation in this process?

Mr. LECOMPTE. Thank you. I think that is absolutely critical, and I think any process that moves forward must not only include the people of Puerto Rico, but it also must move forward a process where there is greater accountability to the people of Puerto Rico from their government itself.

I think that has been a key reason why the Archbishop of San Juan and the other religious leaders have continued to call for public budget transparency in this process. I certainly agree with Mr. Mayer in terms of what he is putting out in terms of bankruptcy is not comprehensive in itself. Bankruptcy is one part of a process that needs to take place just like greater degrees of accountability and transparency.

There are several ways that that can move forward. I think the most important way is one of the actions Congress has already taken, which is being able to provide assistance from the U.S. Treasury and their Office of Technical Assistance, which I think is one of the greatest programs at U.S. Treasury. This in itself can provide Puerto Rico with critical advice to keep their debt stock in good order; but even more importantly, it can create greater accountability mechanisms with the people of Puerto Rico to the government itself.

I think these are very important. I think that on any particular conversation around a fiscal control board or a growth authority for representation, it is absolutely critical that you have equal representation from Puerto Rico, the Federal Government, and certainly the kind of staffing that Mayor Williams has talked about in terms of being able to have the kind of technical expertise to support the process.

Mr. YOUNG. The gentleman's time has expired. Mr. Bishop.

Mr. BISHOP. Thank you. I appreciate the witnesses being here. I actually have four questions. I am going to ask two to Mr. Mayer and two to Mayor Williams. So, let me go with those as we talk about them. But before I do that, Mayor Williams, anyone who can do as much as you did to bring baseball to Washington, I have confidence that we can solve this problem as well. And when there is a big league team in San Juan, then we will have arrived.

And, by the way, that is more important than this issue. Very soon, this committee, with Pierluisi's assistance, is going to be drafting legislation that is going to address the situation in Puerto Rico. There are some questions I think are really important just on the overall level to them.

Mr. Mayer, I am going to ask you for those who advocate simply bankruptcy protection from Puerto Rico, the question is: How will Puerto Rico ever get back into the bond market for financing of infrastructure that they are going to definitely have to have? And those who advocate against bankruptcy, how will Puerto Rico bring recalcitrant creditors to the table to discuss debt restructuring.

Now let me go the other two questions, you can think about that. Mayor Williams, for those who advocate an advisory-type board: How will the government of Puerto Rico convince anybody it is going to follow the board's advice when it appears that the government has already taken sound advice and has ignored that advice. But for those who advocate a strong control board, how will such a board carry out its purpose and have the proper respect for the people of the island and the integrity of their government?

So Mr. Mayer, if I could ask you those first two, and then Mayor Williams.

Mr. MAYER. Thank you, Chairman Bishop. I don't think Puerto Rico will easily recover access to the capital markets if it ever uses Chapter 9. And I think that it will have serious knock-on effects across the country. Just last week, the Chicago Board of Education came to market with an $800 million bond issue. But because of the concerns about Puerto Rico and because Illinois is considering giving Chicago Chapter 9, it could not sell the paper.

So, the history—if you take a look at the last five or six big cases, if you look at Detroit, if you look at the California cases, none of these municipalities has been able to go back to the market unless they have a special structure through a state, as Detroit had through Michigan. This is one of the reasons why we have focused on a restructuring with a creditor vote, a real vote where the bondholders feel they have a chance to vote yes or no, rather than a Chapter 9 which pretends to have a creditor vote but does not really, where creditor votes are not important and are routinely disregarded.

So, in answer to your question, I don't think Puerto Rico will regain access to the capital markets if it is given Chapter 9, that it authorizes the public corporations to do so. Right now, the electric company has access to the capital markets if it implements our deal. It does not need Professor Johnson's government intervention. And that deal is being talked about as a template for the sewer company. You have a limited number of governmental corporations even if they have $20 billion of debt. This process can work out, if you let it do so.

Mr. BISHOP. Let me turn to the Mayor. These are the fundamental questions we have to address as a committee. So, if it is an advisory-type board, based on the record, how do we ensure that it is going to happen? If it is a strong board, how do we ensure that we respect the rights of the people of the government of Puerto Rico?

Mr. WILLIAMS. Congressman, first of all, I am glad you enjoy the games. I appreciate that. But, you know, I spoke at an event——

Mr. BISHOP. Except when they were playing the Mets. Those sucked. But other than that, yes.

Mr. WILLIAMS [continuing]. With Speaker Gingrich, who was one of the leaders in the DC recovery along with President Clinton. What the Speaker and I were talking about is, with a board you really need two things, we keep reiterating to everybody here: you need the control and the oversight. You need to look at the break-even at the government and get it to the right level, but you also need economic growth. And I believe that only a strong board puts you in a position to do that; so I would go with the latter.

That said, it is very important that this board be able to work with people on the ground—everybody from the business community, to the unions, to the pensioners, the teachers, and nongovernmental community—to put in place a vision for recovery. Again, I think in the cities that I have mentioned, you have seen that. And, I think you can see this on the island. I have spoken down in San Juan to the people in the government about this. So what I am saying, I believe strongly.

I believe that this notion that a strong entity is like Darth Vader, and everybody is going to run for the hills. If it is done in conjunction with the people on the ground, in conjunction with the government, I think it can work.

Mr. BISHOP. I think you are all talking about having the right people involved in making those decisions. I think Mr. Garcia was saying the same thing, competency precedes before the incentives that have to be there. I appreciate that very much, and I also thank you for mentioning one of the concepts. This committee has already explored the idea of energy development. Obviously, the energy costs in Puerto Rico are significantly higher than the rest of the country, and it is part of the problem they have with their economic development. If we don't address that at the same time, we are missing an opportunity of what has to be done.

I yield back. Sorry to go over.

Mr. YOUNG. Mrs. Torres.

Mrs. TORRES. Thank you, Mr. Chairman. In 2009, as a new Member of the House in the state of California, I saw the eighth largest economy dwindle down to junk bond status. We had a $15 billion deficit, and it was a very, very difficult time in the state managing finances. The House, the Senate could not agree on cuts or a lot of things that we needed to do.

The one thing that helped us out of that mess was greater transparency. We began to put our budget on the Web site. We began a process of seeking input from citizens all across the state asking: How would you balance your budget? If you were limited to this much money, what would that look like for you and what are your priorities?

And, certainly, there were a lot of difficult votes in that. Today we are seeing the negative part of that with teachers that have left the state, and we are unable to recruit good teachers, and that is something that the current legislature is having to deal with.

Mr. Williams, you were the mayor of Washington when the control board was put in place, correct?

Mr. WILLIAMS. Yes.

Mrs. TORRES. Can you share with us what were some of the positive as well as negative issues that you saw when that board was implemented? And how did the people of Washington, how were the residents able to make opinions and have their voices heard, and the government, how were they—you as a mayor, how was your voice heard?

Mr. WILLIAMS. I came into the control board as a CFO. As a CFO, I thought it was really important, first and foremost, to put our financial affairs in order to create the right kind of organizational systems and financial reporting, just to get to ground zero, very, very important. Then on that basis, restoring fundamental financial operations like paying the bills. I know this sounds ridiculous, but like paying the bills——

Mrs. TORRES. But that was not a priority for you before that, to pay the bills?

Mr. WILLIAMS. Yes, we had lines of people, I mean literally out the door, with receivables demanding to be paid, checks that were not cashed, let alone receivables that were not properly managed and recorded. As we began doing that, I saw there was a need and I thought it was very important to go out to the neighborhoods and give understanding, a briefing to the citizens of the city.

I was just the financial guy. Give a briefing to the citizens of the city about what was going on. The analogy I used was that we were on a really hard road as a city in a really overloaded car that was badly driven and underpowered.

Mrs. TORRES. But what were the positive and the negatives of that board, sir?

Mr. WILLIAMS. One of the positives of the board was that it had the authority to comprehensively deal with all the issues we are talking about——

Mrs. TORRES. Over-riding the authority of the local elected officials?

Mr. WILLIAMS. No, it had the authority to supersede in the breach of decisions of the local officials; but actually as a process, worked in collaboration with the Congress and with the local officials.

Mrs. TORRES. Was there a lot of cooperation from your perspective?

Mr. WILLIAMS. What I was trying to say was I tried to ensure that there was cooperation with the counsel——

Mrs. TORRES. OK. Tried and succeed are two different things. Was there cooperation, yes or no?

Mr. WILLIAMS. Yes, we tried and we succeeded in building cooperation with the local citizenry. The fact that I was elected mayor after representing the control board I think speaks to the rapport I was able to achieve.

Mrs. TORRES. All right. Thank you.

Mr. YOUNG. Thank you. Ms. Velazquez.

Ms. VELAZQUEZ. Thank you, Mr. Chairman, for allowing us to participate in this hearing. I do not have to explain how important this is for all the Puerto Rican Members of Congress. We have families in Puerto Rico. All my family is in Puerto Rico.

As we have stated before, not only are we concerned about the ability of Puerto Rico to restructure its debt, but about the humanitarian crisis that is already unfolding if we do not approach this issue in a comprehensive way. Here we are talking about a financial control board, and reading the wonderful memo that was put together, it says here that in New York, the emergency financial control board reduced a huge deficit by forcing the city to shed 60,000 employees, 20 percent of the workforce. And then it went on to talk about Washington, DC.

Well, let me tell you what Puerto Rico has been doing without a control board. It has raised its sales tax to 11.5 percent, the highest in the Nation; reduced government employment by 13,000 over the last 3 years; and cut expenses by 20 percent. It has also undertaken pension reform, froze collective bargaining agreements, and consolidated hundreds of schools.

And Puerto Rico is already taking emergency measures to avoid defaulting on its general obligation bonds. It has done so by borrowing $400 million from the workers' compensation fund, liquidating assets from pension funds, extending third-party payables to almost $2 billion, and defaulting on junior debts in the outstanding principal amount of $7 billion.

We can keep going down this path, but the truth is that the course is set and there is no turning back for Puerto Rico without help from the U.S. Congress.

Mr. Mayor—Mr. Williams, you are here to discuss how effective the control board was to return DC to manage its financial crisis. I would like to ask you—When a control board was created for Washington, DC, how critical of an issue was the district debt load?

Mr. WILLIAMS. Congresswoman, I am not an expert on the debt, and I do not think I am really here as an expert on the debt. I am really here on the experience of the board in executing a financial recovery and the different aspects we talked about. The situations are different, the debt situation in the District is clearly and markedly different from the debt situation in Puerto Rico.

Ms. VELAZQUEZ. Mr. Johnson, do you believe that given Puerto Rico's debt problem, that a control board alone will permit the island to recover, or does it need a restructuring authority as well? And to go beyond Chapter 9, a broader version of restructuring?

Mr. JOHNSON. I think, Ms. Velazquez, you put it exactly right. Puerto Rico is on a downward path right now with partial debt restructurings, agreements, and so on. The territory will continue on that downward path unless a sharp change is made. I support having a growth authority as part of that change. I think you also should change the fiscal relationship with the Federal Government, which is part of what you are talking about.

And I do think that even in the positive scenarios as growth comes back, that some fair, equitable debt restructuring should be on the table, and the growth authority hopefully will have the power to take that on and to do that in a responsible and equitable way. Yes, I think all of the debt——

Ms. VELAZQUEZ. Thank you. Mr. Johnson, you stated in your testimony that creditors were taking on well-documented risks when they lent to Puerto Rico, and that the biggest danger for Puerto Rico is that there will be no comprehensive debt restructuring. What do you say to those that suggest that it is unfair for creditors to suffer losses due to a potential debt restructuring?

Mr. JOHNSON. In such situations, of course creditors are never happy, nor are the people of Puerto Rico happy. This is not where you want to be. But I have not heard anyone today, or any other day recently, say that there is anything surprising about this situation. I think all of our accounts—we may differ on precisely what happened—but all of our accounts begin 10, 20 years ago at least in terms of the unraveling of public finances in Puerto Rico.

Mr. MAYER. Two years ago——

Ms. VELAZQUEZ. And my understanding is that the hedge funds that bought the totality of Puerto Rico's bond issuers in 2014 did so without current audited financial statements. So, for those who are saying that Puerto Rico does not provide the type of statements that are necessary, they knew prior to buying those bonds the financial conditions of Puerto Rico.

Mr. MAYER. Congresswoman——

Mr. YOUNG. Gentleman, time is up. Mr. Gutierrez.

Mr. GUTIERREZ. Thank you so much, Mr. Chairman, Ranking Member, and Resident Commissioner Pierluisi, for allowing me to participate today.

I just wanted to make a few points, and that is—I am just going to go back to the memorandum that was issued to everyone here. At the end of the second paragraph on background it says, "Congress retains plenary authority under Article 4, Section 3, Clause 2 of the U.S. Constitution to determine the ultimate disposition of the political status of Puerto Rico."

The fact is that the Congress of the United States retains plenary powers over everything in Puerto Rico, not just the status of Puerto Rico. That is fundamentally what should be at issue, too, at this hearing, because you cannot resolve one without the other. You want to take the government of Puerto Rico that does not control how merchandise is brought in or out because the Jones Act says we must use the U.S. Merchant Marines.

We are not going to discuss that here today, tomorrow, or any time between now and March 31. Yet the consumers in Puerto Rico need—you want to talk about economic development? How do you have economic development if your energy is outlandishly expensive and if you do not invest in making sure that you have a clear water supply on a tropical island?

So look, there are a lot of things, but fundamentally let's deal with one thing because the background statement does not say it.

Why don't we all come to the conclusion which I am sure Mr. Pierluisi agrees with as the Resident Commissioner of Puerto Rico? Puerto Rico is a colony of the United States of America. Puerto Rico is war booty from the war in 1898. How did Puerto Rico become part of the United States of America? It was not like the Puerto Ricans all got together one day, held a convention and said would you allow us. No. It was military intervention in Puerto Rico.

Now, I would like to say to the Resident Commissioner—I agree, and I am going to fight with you to maintain some sense of reliability between what we do here and the functioning of the people of Puerto Rico over their future. But I fear that we might be trying to make a distinction without a difference in that the truth is that in Puerto Rico we do not control any of the basic things. We do not control who comes to the island or who leaves the island because that is controlled by the Federal Government.

Our court system? No, you simply appeal to the Supreme Court. I mean you simply send it to a Federal court and the Supreme Court of the United States, and the laws that we pass here. So when people say, oh, the people of Puerto Rico, they are responsible for everything that happened bad there and they need to take responsibility—no, the Congress of the United States has to assume responsibility over Puerto Rico because we have, as is stated here, plenary powers over the people of Puerto Rico.

Why are we having this hearing here? And why aren't they having it in Puerto Rico? Because they cannot have it there because they do not have those plenary powers. So look, I am concerned about senior citizens, Mr. Mayer. I am hopeful that the Franklin Fund has diversified their funds to the point because I do not want you to make it sound like the only thing in that fund are Puerto Rican bonds because they are not. I checked before I came to this hearing. You are a very well diversified fund, and I hope you fulfilled your fiduciary responsibilities to the people that you sold the bonds to and informed them of the precarious situation of the very bonds that you were purchasing.

So, don't put on us the responsibility of something that you sold to senior citizens. OK? Make sure that you understand that you, too, have a responsibility as the market in the United States of America. I just want to say, look, everything is different in Puerto Rico. Everything is. You cannot even go to McDonald's. The menu is in Spanish. Everything is different, because Puerto Rico belongs to, but is not a part of the United States of America.

And I am not saying that. That is what the Supreme Court of the United States of America has stated. Puerto Rico is a colony of the United States. There is no way around it. Otherwise we would not be here and the statement as made by the committee very ably that we have plenary powers over Puerto Rico.

Here is what I would suggest. Number one, let's restructure this debt, fully. It is not a state. I did not come here to try to make Puerto Rico more like a state. I came here to make the Puerto Rican people whole so that they could have a future. Let's restore the ability of the people of Puerto Rico to invite people to Puerto Rico. Let's stop fighting over what is the reality of Puerto Rico and what they need.

Last, Mr. Chairman, can't we provide the people of Puerto Rico the incentives to create jobs, jobs, jobs? Economic activity instead of expansion of more welfare programs in Puerto Rico? What we need is jobs so that the people of Puerto Rico can use their intelligence, because when the people of Puerto Rico leave and vanish from that island to come to the United States of America, guess what they do, they come here to work because they are bright, intelligent people.

Let the Congress of the United States take the heel off the people of Puerto Rico and let them live prosperously. Let them have the economic development that they so deserve. Thank you very much, Mr. Chairman, and thank you for having these hearings. I look for a resolution by March 31 of this year, as Speaker Ryan has so promised.

Mr. YOUNG. Mr. Serrano. Sorry, you were first here and had to be the last. I do apologize.

Mr. SERRANO. That's OK, Mr. Chairman. And thank you and all the other committee leaders for allowing the three non-members of the committee to participate. I was very interested in Mr. Gutierrez's statement. I am not going to say that he says the same thing I have been saying; that would be unfair. But it sounded similar to something I have been saying all along, which is what we are doing here is putting a Band-Aid on a larger problem.

The problem is the status of Puerto Rico. As long as Puerto Rico is a colony of the United States, these kinds of issues will recur, and recur, and recur. The only solution is to resolve the political status—117 years is a long, long time for Puerto Rico to be a colony, and it is about time that it ended. I am supportive of anything that ends the colonial status, as long as the people who are much better than I on this issue come to me and say Puerto Rico is no longer a territory of the United States, then whatever the change is, I will be fine with. I think I am hearing more and more folks who were opposed to change saying we do not have the power, therefore we need change, and that is very important.

Mr. Williams, Mayor Williams, I lived with you the whole time. I was Chairman and Ranking Member of the subcommittee, the first subcommittee on appropriations when DC was a committee by itself. You recall those days. Then you became part of financial services, where I am Ranking Member now. And I have to tell you, when Members spoke to us within ourselves, which we often do regardless of what the public thinks, you got a lot of credit for what happened in DC because you did something that should not be lost on this argument, this hearing, which is you demanded respect for Washington with a control board, but you were willing to work with the Federal Government to resolve the problem. Let me repeat that. You demanded respect.

And I remember you in front of us at the committee hearing saying you are asking me to do something that is not dignified for the people of Washington, DC, while understanding that you had to work with us. And many, many people said at that time, Members of Congress, we are not crazy about DC. DC has always been the place that people beat up on. I think the history books will say that, besides the Nationals, you did a lot for this city during that period of time, and I applaud you for that.

But incidentally, Mr. Chairman, all the city council members who gave him a hard time about the Nationals showed up on opening day because I was there, and they were taking credit for it.

Mr. Mayer, I am a little confused. According to my information—and you correct me if I am wrong—you are a member of the National Bankruptcy Conference. Is that correct?

Mr. MAYER. That is correct.

Mr. SERRANO. But the conference supports Chapter 9 extension to Puerto Rico, and you do not.

Mr. MAYER. That is also correct. I abstained from the debate at the conference on that topic, and my views are not the views of the conference.

Mr. SERRANO. OK. And the conference knows that you are testifying or that you disagree with them and are testifying in that way saying that you do not support Chapter 9 while the conference does?

Mr. MAYER. That is correct, yes.

Mr. SERRANO. OK. Mr. Chairman, just a note. Our biggest challenge will not be finding a solution or getting what Speaker Ryan has promised to take place. It is going back to the same issue of how do you give the territory the needed assistance while not making it more of a colony. Not more colonialism. And you are going to have Members of Congress who are not going to think that way, who are going to say if they are going to get help, they have to pay.

An oversight board is fine. The Resident Commissioner has said that oversight is fine. Oversight exists already. Every single dollar that goes to Puerto Rico, or to any state, or to any municipality, you have to answer to the Federal Government for it. You have to answer to the Appropriations Committee for it. That should be the case. But to bring Puerto Rico to its knees when it is already on one knee would just be adding more pain to a situation that is very painful.

I find myself in a unique situation. I was born in the colony and now I am a Member of Congress of the group that holds the colony, and so sometimes I think Puerto Ricans need a national psychiatrist to deal with this issue of how we deal with both issues at once. I mean we love the place we were born in, we love the place whose Army we served in and we grew up in. I came to New York when I was 7 years old.

But I think it is about time that the place I was raised in solve the issue of the place I was born in. And I think you could go a long way, because, Mr. Chairman, you have been a very strong supporter. You have gone a step forward, above and beyond. You have actually asked for statehood for Puerto Rico.

The strongest point you have made is that you want change, dignity, and respect; and I thank you for that both as an American and as an American who was born in Puerto Rico and one who lived in Alaska. By the way, this may be a hearing about Puerto Rico, but you notice it has gotten colder as the hearing went on. That is the influence of the Alaskan Chairman. Thank you, Mr. Chairman.

Mr. YOUNG. Thank you, Mr. Serrano. I appreciate it.

Mr. Garcia, in your testimony, you cite the powers and tools that should be vested with the authority. Focused on the first bullet point in that section of your testimony—implement structural reforms in the government of Puerto Rico and its political subdivision—why do you feel it is necessary that this is a power of the authority? Is the current or future government of Puerto Rico able to make the necessary structural reforms on its own?

Mr. GARCIA. Mr. Chairman, based on my experience during 2009 and 2011, there was always a lot of great political will to be able to go and do the restructuring, but it is always a very hard process to be agreed upon. Lots of analysis, lots of conversations happened. One of the things that we were not able to achieve on the control board was to be able to affect good reforms in the structure of the government of Puerto Rico.

So, I think this is a great, unique opportunity based on a Federal control board that will be seeking both interests, not only the fiscal, but the economic part to finally be able to analyze the situation and work with the people of Puerto Rico to implement a government that will work for its people in a very efficient and agile manner.

Mr. YOUNG. Thank you. Mr. Mayer, you mentioned the energy board has reached an agreement, negotiated with the bondholders. Is that correct?

Mr. MAYER. Yes, Mr. Chairman.

Mr. YOUNG. Why does the legislature have to approve that?

Mr. MAYER. The agreement is structured in a way where the debt moves off the balance sheet of the electric company and onto a special purpose vehicle which is paid out of a cents per kilowatt hour charge. That has to be established by legislation. It could be established by an authority, but it has to be established by legislation.

And the result of this transaction is that the total debt load goes down. The total amount of debt goes down by 15 percent, the interest rate drops, and there is a 5-year holiday on principal repayments. So, hundreds of millions of dollars in cash flow are freed up for the electric company to make the investment in natural gas and other plants that need to be made. And this requires the Puerto Rican legislature to change Puerto Rican law so that it all works.

Measures have been before the legislature now for probably a month and a half, 2 months, and the deadline for having it passed has already been extended by the bondholders. Every day that goes by without passing this legislation probably costs in interest rate relief alone $250,000 a day, because that is the amount of relief that would happen. So, if the legislature passes the law, then this restructuring can go forward that will save everybody a lot of money and it will make capital available to PREPA to make the investments that need to be made.

Mr. YOUNG. I am concerned that energy is what drives the economy. The energy of Puerto Rico is extremely high. That is something we are going to have to address somewhere in this Congress, too, that either we go nuclear, which Puerto Ricans may not want, natural gas can possibly work, restructure is extremely expensive. It is something we are going to have to look at.

I am going to yield to the Resident Commissioner, 2 minutes for his time to make a statement or ask a question.

Mr. PIERLUISI. Thank you so much, Chairman—Chairman Young, Chairman Bishop, all of those present at this hearing, I believe that we should put the blame game aside. I believe that we should do all we can to transcend partisan politics.

And I believe that we should come up with a legislative package for Puerto Rico that makes sense, given the crisis Puerto Rico is facing, given the status of Puerto Rico, and given the reality that this is not a foreign country or foreign nationals. You are talking about American citizens who can hop on a plane from one day to the next if the going is tough down there and nobody can blame them.

I can say this with credibility because on the one hand I represent all of the American citizens living in Puerto Rico in this Congress. In addition, I chair the New Progressive Party of Puerto Rico, the pro-statehood party of Puerto Rico. And I am running for governor.

And yet, I am saying we need to assist the current administration of Puerto Rico. We need to give the government of Puerto Rico the necessary tools to put its fiscal house in order and to, yes, restructure its debts. Now ideally, we should do that on a negotiated basis, on a consensual basis. But it is not happening. It has not happened for too long. So, the concept of having a board that would assist Puerto Rico in getting its fiscal house in order, and that would have a key role in promoting the restructuring and facilitating the debt restructuring, makes sense.

And to the extent states do not have that tool, I should say I am the first one who does not like the current status of Puerto Rico, but I have to recognize that Congress does have plenary power over the territory of Puerto Rico. That is why this committee has primary jurisdiction over this issue. So, that is the challenge.

Chairman, I believe we can work it out. We can provide Puerto Rico the tools to get back on a path to recovery, get its fiscal house in order, and in the process be fair to creditors, both institutional and individual, including my constituents. Thank you.

Mr. YOUNG. I thank the gentleman. I can only say that I have listened to Mr. Serrano and yourself and the other witnesses. If we had done what I said 15 years ago that we should have, we would not be here today. And I would like to suggest, respectfully, we are trying to solve an immediate problem which is serious and that does not stop me from still pushing statehood. I know there is no chance in—can I say hell in this committee—no chance in hell of that happening——

Mr. PIERLUISI. Say heck.

Mr. YOUNG [continuing]. Under the present climate. But that does not preclude this from coming up again if everybody gets their house in order, and that is what we are going to try to do. I want to thank the witnesses. This is one of the best panels I have been able to be Chair of. You had good ideas and good thoughts, and with your permission we will probably call on you for a little bit of sage advice. As I mentioned before what will happen if we don't, and we will do the best we can. With that, if there are no other comments, this meeting is adjourned.

[Whereupon, at 12:51 p.m., the subcommittee was adjourned.]

[LIST OF DOCUMENTS SUBMITTED FOR THE RECORD RETAINED IN THE
COMMITTEE'S OFFICIAL FILES]

—April 14, 2011, Carlos Garcia, Junta De Restructuración Y Estabilización Fiscal, Letter and proposal submitted to Governor Luis G. Fortuno, Hon. Jennifer Gonzalez Rico, and Hon. Thomas Rivera Schatz. 39 pages.

—December 1, 2015, James E. Spiotto, "Is Chapter 9 Bankruptcy the Ultimate Remedy for Financially Distressed Territories and Sovereigns Such as Puerto Rico: Are There Better Resolution Mechanisms?" Testimony submitted to U.S. Senate Committee on the Judiciary. 54 pages.

—December 1, 2015, James E. Spiotto, PowerPoint Presentation, "Lessons Learned From Financially Distressed Governments and A Resulting Proposed Sovereign Recovery Debt Adjustment Mechanism." Presentation submitted to U.S. Senate Committee on the Judiciary. 146 pages.

—February 2, 2016, Congresswoman Stacey E. Plaskett, Statement submitted to House Committee on Natural Resources, Subcommittee on Indian, Insular, and Alaska Native Affairs. 3 pages.

—February 2, 2016, James E. Spiotto, Testimony submitted to Chairman Young regarding the establishment of a Puerto Rico Financial Stability and Economic Growth Authority. 12 pages.

—February 2, 2016, Ricardo Rossello, PhD, Statement submitted to House Committee on Natural Resources, Subcommittee on Indian, Insular, and Alaska Native Affairs. 10 pages.

—February 2, 2016, Mike Orr, Sitnasuak Native Corporation, Testimony submitted to Chairman Young and House Committee on Natural Resources, Subcommittee on Indian, Insular, and Alaska Native Affairs. 2 pages.

—February 2, 2016, Miriam J. Ramirez, MD, Statement submitted to House Committee on Natural Resources, Subcommittee on Indian, Insular, and Alaska Native Affairs. 3 pages.

—February 25, 2016, Arnaldo Vargas-Nin, Statement submitted to House Committee on Natural Resources. 4 pages.

○